Learning to Make Toast

Kelly Sharp

Published by BookLocker.com, Inc., St. Petersburg, Florida, U.S.A.

Printed on acid-free paper.

BookLocker.com, Inc.
2017

First Edition

To Nadine, Joan's (Edith's) co-conspirator

Table of Contents

The Crash

It wasn't supposed to end like this. She had finally begun to get it right. She had left behind the crime, the drugs and most of the drinking. Now, she was living a fairy tale life, complete with loving husband, new house, even a dog. Joan had finally found the kind of future she had always longed for.

Then the fairy tale ended.

Joan Miller and John, her husband of seven years, were in Ogden, Utah, in June 1999, to celebrate her 42nd birthday at a leadership conference. Looking forward to a weekend of fun, friendship and learning, they had no reason to think this day would be different from yesterday or the day before that. But it was. This was the day of the crash, the day when everything changed—when her old life ended and her new one began.

The unsuspecting Millers arrived in Ogden with just enough time to get to their hotel, touch base with old friends and head over to the Dee Events Center for the evening entertainment. Dressed in the new green suit and black pumps she had purchased specifically for this trip, Joan sprinted to the front of the auditorium to beat the thousands of other attendees to a front row seat to see the band Dreamer.

The manager of the arena yelled at her for running, but the outgoing and enthusiastic Joan laughed off his warnings. She was there to have fun, which meant being right up front. John could only chuckle as he lovingly watched his wife of seven years dancing near the stage and taking a turn at the microphone singing with the band. This was his cheerleader, full of energy and eager to share her excitement with everyone around her.

John and Joan stayed until the end of the show, said good night to their friends and jumped into their rented Ford Escort for the short drive back to their room at the Ramada Inn. It took about 10 minutes for John to realize they were lost.

"I made a wrong turn. I turned left instead of right," he says. As Joan teased him for missing the turn, he decided to head for a nearby gas station and ask for directions back to their hotel. They never saw the drunk driver in the Toyota Tacoma flying up behind them at 75 miles per hour. The Tacoma rear ended their car, spinning it across the center median into the path of a Chrysler sedan with three people inside.

From the passenger seat, Joan could see the sedan heading straight for them and knew they were going to get hit again. "Joan was making this sound," John remembers, his voice breaking. "She saw it coming and was making an animal type noise. It seemed to take a long time, but I'm sure it was just a few seconds. Just after we got hit the second time, I thought to myself over and over, 'If we don't flip over, we will be OK.' I just kept thinking that."

As the cars collided, the second impact sent their Escort spinning and skidding down the road, where it finally came to a stop just outside the center lane.

The drunk driver in the Toyota Tacoma didn't stop.

Fighting to Live

When the car finally stopped spinning and the dust settled John could hear people yelling for someone to call 911. He looked over at his wife and felt his heart stop. The passenger side of the car, where Joan had been sitting, had taken the brunt of the second impact. Her head had slammed repeatedly into the door frame.

"I looked over and saw Joan with her head up against the window barely breathing," John says. He could see her hands twitching in her lap and blood coming from her left ear. Desperate to get to her, John reached for his door handle, only to realize he couldn't move. In his panic about Joan, he didn't realize he had a chest injury and had wrenched muscles in his back and groin. Trapped in his seat, frantic that he couldn't get Joan to respond, he didn't know what to do to help her.

"I felt I had to do something, so I took her seatbelt off," he says. "I guess I was thinking it would make it easier for the EMT's."

The paramedics arrived quickly; one working to get John out of the car and into the waiting ambulance while the others went to work on Joan.

"I was very cold, freezing," John remembers. "I asked several times how Joan was and they said, 'Oh she's fine'—which is just what they say." Trying to keep him from worrying, one rescuer even suggested that John go to a different hospital than the trauma one Joan was headed to because it would be less expensive. John thanked him for the offer but declined. He would go wherever Joan went.

John may have been reassured by the paramedics' calm, professional demeanor, but the reality was that they were frantically trying to extricate and stabilize Joan just enough to get her safely into the ambulance. Her chances of survival were dropping by the moment. They raced her to the emergency department at McKay-Dee Hospital Center in Ogden, where Blake G. Welling, MD, a board-certified neurosurgeon was on duty.

Looking at her skull fracture, the massive laceration on her head and the blood coming from her nose and ears, Dr. Welling had little hope that he could keep her alive, much less that she would someday recover. He was particularly concerned about her fixed and dilated pupils.

"Pupils should be the same size," Dr. Welling said. Joan's right pupil was *blown*, which is when the black part of the pupil expands to cover the iris, the colored part of eye. To a neurosurgeon, this is an indication of significant brain damage.

Because of Joan's extensive injuries, Dr. Welling had Joan in surgery within 15 minutes of entering the emergency department and began the frantic process of trying to save her. He started by working on the open, depressed skull fracture that had driven more than 20 shards of shattered bone, dirt, and debris into the right parietal lobe of her brain, the area responsible for movement and sensation on the left side of the body.

As he removed the bone splinters, he also removed the surrounding damaged tissue and drained the blood pooling in her skull. He then covered the open area in her skull with the remaining skin, leaving a lemon-sized hole in her head. "She had a soft spot," Dr. Welling says. "It's like taking a 5 iron and taking a divot out of your head."

After the surgery, Dr. Welling used the Glasgow Coma Scale (GCS) to score Joan on her ability to open her eyes and respond verbally, as well as on her motor responsiveness, to determine the seriousness of her coma. The results were not encouraging.

According to Dr. Welling, the best GCS rating after a head injury is a 15. If the patient scores a 15, it means she is awake, alert and oriented to the world around her. Although she may have a minor concussion, the prognosis for recovery is excellent. In other words the lower the score, the more difficult the recovery.

"The worst you can get is a 3," Dr. Welling explains. "People who are dead get a GCS of 3. ... When people have a Glasgow score of 3, 4 or 5, we are talking about a mortality rate over 97%. The other 3% are left in a vegetative state." When he evaluated her, Joan had a GCS of 4. This confirmed his diagnosis that Joan had only occasional brain stem responses. Her prognosis was poor.

Dr. Welling transferred Joan to the ICU, where another set of doctors began treating the broken bones in her face and pelvis, and went to deliver his devastating diagnosis to John.

John, waiting in the emergency department for treatment of his own injuries, had no idea his beloved Joan was close to death. He knew her injuries were severe, but it never dawned on him that he might lose her. He was in the middle of an interview with a police officer about the accident when Dr. Welling came into his room. At first, John couldn't quite grasp what Dr. Welling was trying to tell him.

"He told me that Joan had a skull fracture," John says. "Not being a medical person, and being so literal sometimes, I thought, '*Fracture* means *crack*—big deal.' I said, 'She'll be OK, right?' The look on the doctor's face was shock. He obviously didn't know what to say."

Patiently, Dr. Welling described the seriousness of Joan's condition and prepared John for the high chance that she wouldn't make it through the night. Even if Joan did live, he explained to John, her injury was so devastating that she might never wake up.

"It was at that point that I got tunnel vision," John remembers, his voice cracking with pain. "Someone came in and asked if I wanted to call someone, and I asked them to call my sister, Shawn. I didn't talk to Shawn very long. She asked if I wanted her to come, and I said, 'Yes,' and that was the end of that conversation."

After Dr. Welling left the room, the medical staff began treating John's injuries, splinting his broken ankle and easing his punctured lung by relieving the pressure through a tube in his chest.

"It felt like they used a railroad spike that they heated up first and shoved in my ribs. I had never experienced any pain like that. It was really intense."

The double whammy of learning his wife might die and enduring his own medical treatment overwhelmed him.

"After that, I don't remember anything until the next morning."

The Family Arrives

The phone rang at 5 a.m., waking John's sister, Shawn, at her home in Portland, Ore.

"It's that phone call you never expect to get," Shawn says. "The nurse was very calm, and she said, 'I've called to tell you that your brother and sister-in-law have been in a serious automobile accident. John is in serious condition, and Joan is in grave condition.' When I asked for a definition of 'grave' she said, 'Joan is not expected to survive.'"

Shawn immediately asked to talk to her brother, and the nurse handed him the phone. "When Johnny came on the phone, his words were 'Please come. Joan is really bad.'"

After calling the rest of both families to tell them the horrible news, she and her sister Kim caught the first available flight to Utah. Meeting up with Joan's sister Lisa and her husband Chris, they were at John's side when Dr. Welling came to give him an update him on Joan's prognosis. Delivering the horrible news that she might not make it, Dr. Welling also encouraged them not to give up hope.

"He said, 'She may surprise us' and I said 'Joan is good at surprises,'" John remembers. "I was still in denial, not knowing at all what the severity of the injury was."

Much of John's refusal to accept Dr. Welling's prognosis came simply from not having seen her. His own injuries were so severe that his doctor had refused to allow him to leave his hospital bed. All John had was the memory of the paramedics taking Joan away in the ambulance. He knew she was hurt, but she was alive, so he was convinced she was going to be fine. He simply couldn't accept Dr. Welling's chilling words as anything more than a worst case scenario for someone else. It was impossible that Dr. Welling was talking about Joan.

Finally, after two long days, John was allowed to take the trip to the ICU to see Joan. "I wasn't prepared at all for her appearance. At all. That was a shock," he says. The person lying unresponsive in that hospital bed—hooked up to a ventilator and a feeding tube, covered in IVs and wrapped in bandages and casts—couldn't possibly be his Joan.

Shawn says, "Johnny was in a lot of physical pain with his own injuries and could not put any weight at all on his leg, and he had the tube in his chest. Our sister Kim and I tried to prepare him for Joan's appearance, but when he actually saw her he came out of that wheelchair and covered the last two feet to her bedside in sound and motion that were pure anguish. It tore me up."

John finally understood what Dr. Welling had been trying to tell him. This bruised and battered stranger was his wife, his one true love, and she was fighting for her life. Even if she lived, she might never really come back to him. Brokenhearted, all John could do was wait.

Although Dr. Welling tried to keep John's hopes up, he says he did not have high expectations for Joan's future. Even if she somehow survived, the damage to the right parietal lobe of her brain could be devastating.

"I never hear about most of these patients again, especially those from out of state," he says. "I can only assume they end up in a skilled nursing facility for the rest of their lives."

Luckily, Dr. Welling underestimated Joan. While her family braced themselves for the news that she had died, Joan had other plans.

"When Kim and I first got to Utah, Joan was still in ICU, still in a coma, still had all these tubes, and her head was swollen," Shawn says. "I knew Kim didn't think she was going to make it. But when I walked into that room, I was slapped with so much energy that I knew she was in there and ready to come back out. It was just a matter of time."

Shawn believes the energy she felt had to be coming directly from Joan, because when she left the room, she no longer felt it. "Every time we would go up there, the energy would hit me sooner. At last, the energy was at the elevators; it was moving out," she says. In her mind, this meant Joan was still in there, trying to reach them and fighting her way back.

John also never lost hope. He knew Joan would come back to him. He wasn't going to lose her.

"Three or four days after the accident," Shawn says, "Johnny and I went to see the neurosurgeon, and he said, 'You know, if Joan comes out of the coma she will likely be in a vegetative state.' Johnny said, 'You don't know Joan.'"

Joan spent four days in a medically induced coma to allow her body to rest before the doctors decided to try to wake her up. Bringing her out of the coma would allow them to determine if she had any brain function left and determine her chances of recovery. Much to their surprise, Joan immediately showed signs she had no intention of giving up.

"The doctor was pinching her, over and over, trying to get a response, and they asked her to wiggle her fingers," Shawn remembers. "Joan flipped him off. That's when we knew she was still in there."

Joan had survived, but would she really recover? Would she still be Joan? Would she have a future? Only time would tell.

Joan Wakes

When Joan finally opened her eyes, an announcement went across the PA system at McKay-Dee Hospital letting everyone know she was awake and a wave of applause and cheering broke out. Given the severity of her injuries, members of the hospital staff, as well as attendees of the leadership conference had closely followed her progress.

"The hospital had to assign someone to keep people away, because strangers from all over the country who attended the conference wanted to come pray over me," Joan says. Her supporters were thrilled by the news that she had woken up. Now the question was: What happens next?

When Joan thinks back to first opening her eyes, her memories are of confusion. She knew she was in a hospital, because she could see medical equipment and could feel pain in her arm and leg, but nothing else made sense.

Looking at the people standing around her bed, she struggled to figure out who they were. She knew they were familiar, but couldn't quite grasp names or relationships. Most concerning, she couldn't figure out why she was lying in a hospital bed and why her voice and her eyes didn't seem to want to work.

"I was really confused as to why the few words coming out of my mouth were *garbledy gook*, and I couldn't at all figure out what was wrong with my eyes, why I couldn't see clearly," she recalls. "That was my biggest worry. I couldn't figure out why those two things didn't work."

It didn't take her long to figure out John was sitting beside the bed stroking her leg. Then she saw Shawn next to him. As her mind cleared, she slowly began to recognize the other members of her family around her bed and the different sense of energy each brought with them.

Shawn brought calmness, and her mother, Rosemary, conveyed love and support. Kim, the police officer, provided a sense of strength and security, and her sister, Tina, meant comfort, because of her medical background.

"As whacked out as I was, I remember those feelings," Joan said. "These were the most important people to have at my side when I was waking up. I knew I was okay to sleep."

For days, Joan slipped in and out of consciousness as she fought her way back to the world. Her awareness of her surroundings might have been shaky, but feeling John rubbing her leg each time she woke grounded her to reality.

"As long as he was touching me, I knew I was going to be OK," Joan says.

Her doctors were cautiously optimistic about Joan's progress, her ability to follow commands, move her arms and legs, and balance next to her bed just 10 short days after the crash. One even noted on June 22, "Overall, her recovery has been remarkable in that she presented with a Glasgow Coma Score of 4."

John, on the other hand, struggled to see anything remarkable. For him, Joan's recovery consisted of a never-ending series of shocks as her condition became clearer.

As the doctors applauded Joan's ability to stand on her own as a triumph, all John saw was his wife struggling to hold herself upright. "They got her up and out of bed, and she was having a hard time maintaining her balance. She was leaning forward and side to side. But they got her up, with a walker and someone on each side. She walked maybe 10 feet and went back to bed. It was all she could do," he says.

While the doctors were encouraged by what they defined as a good grasp of reality for someone with a brain injury, John saw a wife who didn't always remember him. The doctors saw someone who recovered quickly from a brief bout of pneumonia from her time on the ventilator; he saw his wife struggling to breathe. Each day seemed to bring a new bout of bad news or challenges just to keep her stabilized.

John also struggled with the changes in his beloved wife's appearance. With her bald head, an eye that pointed up to the sky, a huge dent in her skull and bruises from head to toe, she looked deformed. She no longer looked like his Joan. Even removing some of the bandages didn't help.

"After they took the bandages off her head, and the swelling had gone down a little bit, you could see this spot, a flat spot. It was another one of those little shocks you don't expect," he remembers sadly.

As the days went on, Joan slowly continued to improve physically, but mentally she remained confused. She knew it was hard to talk and that she couldn't quite focus her eyes, but she had no idea why.

The brain injury she suffered left her unable to process what was going on around her. She didn't know they were in Utah, why she was in the hospital or how old she was. She often couldn't remember the names of the people around her bed or in her room, including the name of the man she knew as her husband. She didn't even realize she had nerve damage in her arm. *And she didn't care.*

The Joan who opened her eyes in Utah four days after the crash didn't know she had any problems. She believed she was the same person she had always been and couldn't understand why everyone around her kept insisting there was some kind of problem. For Joan, waking up in Utah was like waking in a parallel universe where everything had changed.

"I don't really remember my life before. I know I had one but I don't feel connected to it." she explains. "I've always been like this. I hadn't changed. They had."

This challenge to make sense of her world would haunt Joan throughout her recovery. Discovering and accepting the kind of person she had been before the crash would be even more disconcerting.

Who Was She?

It wasn't surprising to find Joan Miller involved in a drunk driving crash. What *was* surprising was that she hadn't caused it. Alcohol, bad decisions and Joan were friends from long before, and if circumstances had been different, her story could have had another ending. Instead of becoming a living miracle and public speaker, she could have been responsible for ending someone else's life. It took a drunk driver and a traumatic brain injury to finally make her the person she was meant to be.

Joan, the fourth of six daughters born to Lester and Rosemary Cornely, grew up in a three-story, white-and-red brick house in the Reed College Heights neighborhood of Portland, Ore. They were a close, tightknit, Catholic family, living in a home filled with love, laughter and chaos. Rosemary ran a dressmaking shop in the basement, and Lester worked as a CPA. The children's days were full of school, music lessons and church.

Joan decided at an early age that she wanted to follow her mom's entrepreneurial example, so she learned to sew, scoring her first paying customer while still in grade school. She and her mother would spend hours in fabric stores choosing patterns and fabric, then head home to sew together in the basement shop.

For the six children, the anticipation of holidays ruled the household, and Rosemary and Lester never missed an opportunity to make them special for their girls.

"We always colored Easter eggs and hid them. Every year, Mama made us matching Easter dresses to wear to mass. Daddy was soo proud as he stood at the end of the pew with his wife and six daughters in their matching dresses and new black, patent-leather shoes filled up an entire pew."

"Mama made homemade donuts for us every Halloween. After Halloween, we'd each put our candy in a brown bag, put our name on it and then put it into the freezer in the basement. We got to eat one piece of candy after dinner every night until it was gone."

"When we were little, we'd have a small Christmas tree in the basement along with the big one in the living room," Joan remembers fondly. "There is a fireplace downstairs, so we also had to have a tree there for Santa to leave stuff for us. And of course, Santa never let us down. There were a few presents down there along with the rest of the haul in the living room."

Joan started high school in 1972 at St. Mary's Academy, a Catholic high school, where her childhood friend Kathy Richard remembers her as a social butterfly. "If you think about the most popular person in the whole high school that was Joan. Think bubbly, fun, funny, lively, effervescent, cute as can be," Kathy says. "Think of Jennifer Aniston, just a bubbly, likable person. Nobody didn't like Joan."

Joan seemed the typical, popular teenage girl. Cheerleader, Drum and Bugle Corps, coach of the grade school softball team; Joan could be found everywhere. "I only went to school for the social environment," she says. "I didn't go there to learn."

That social life came with a dark underside of drugs, alcohol and constant partying. Speed was Joan's drug of choice, and her fake ID gave her ample access to alcohol in local bars and stores. She routinely kept vodka in her school locker to mix with Coke as she went from class to class.

According to Kathy, much of this was part of the culture of the times. "Everyone drank," she says. "All our parents were partying every weekend. I was around a lot of adults who were drinking, and it was considered acceptable."

The norm in those years consisted of parties every weekend, social drinking and having one more for the road. Drug and alcohol prevention, DUI laws, DARE programs and studies of the effects of alcohol on the brain were in their infancy. Society viewed teenage partying as a rite of passage, just a normal part of growing up. Unlike many troubled teens of today who mask issues at home with drugs and alcohol, Joan had no external reason for her drinking. "I wasn't trying to escape anything," she says. "I had a great home life. I was just being social."

High school friend Mara Windstar agrees. "It was the '70's," she says. Drugs and alcohol had not found the societal disapproval that would be common 30 years later. It was not unusual to have students under the influence, even in a Catholic high school. And Joan's abuse was well known to her schoolmates. "I really wasn't surprised," Mara says when she later learned about the severity of Joan's addictions. Joan may have thought she was hiding her use, but she wasn't fooling anyone.

For many of those partying teens, drinking led to sex, and the result surprised the naive Joan. She says that her first wakeup call about her behavior should have been at 17, when she went to Planned Parenthood to get on the pill, only to be told she was already pregnant.

"The pregnancy was from the first guy I had ever had sex with," Joan says. "I knew nothing about sex or pregnancy and believed everything he told me about how it wouldn't happen. I trusted him."

They had already broken up by the time she thought about the need for birth control. Although she liked him, it was an impulsive, superficial relationship. "We would drink and screw," Joan says, describing the first of many poor alcohol- and drug-based decisions. Their breakup came from issues of distance rather than emotion.

"He lived in a different town, and it was too far away for us to continue seeing each other," Joan said.

Until her trip to Planned Parenthood, Joan had no clue that she was pregnant. For five months, she had explained her lack of periods as the erratic behavior of a teenage body and her morning sickness as a lengthy case of the flu. But when the test results came back positive, she knew she had to make plans for her child's future.

"I knew at that moment I would give the baby up for adoption," she says. "I was too young to be a mother, and my baby needed parents."

Terrified about how her devoutly Catholic parents were going to take the news that their unmarried, teenage daughter was pregnant, Joan asked her eldest sister, Tina, to come with her for support when she dropped the bombshell. Although shocked and disappointed, her parents surprised her.

"My dad took me out to dinner the next night to tell me they loved me, everything would be all right, and they supported my decision to give the baby up for adoption. They only asked that it go to a Catholic family. I felt that was the least I could do, so I agreed," Joan says.

Now Joan needed to face her new boyfriend Tom. Their relationship was only a few months old and Joan was head over heels in love. Telling him she was pregnant with another man's child broke her heart. She had no idea how he would take the news. But like her parents, Tom surprised her. He said he would stand by her, supporting her throughout her pregnancy and in her decision to give the baby to an adoptive family.

Overwhelmed and overjoyed by the response and support from those who loved her, Joan had one last hurdle to clear. She desperately wanted to stay in school throughout her pregnancy to finish her education, even though there was little chance of that happening. In 1974, society considered pregnant teenagers a threat to the morality of other girls and often required that unwed mothers be hidden at an *Aunt Fannie's* in another town until after the birth of the baby.

Preparing for the worst, Joan and her parents were already planning ahead, deciding it would be best if she stayed at Tina's house to protect her from the inevitable neighborhood gossip and the condemnation of the Catholic church. To their shock, the church had a surprise in store. The nuns at St. Mary's were supportive of her desire to stay in school while pregnant.

"I was astonished that they let her," Kathy says. "It was a Catholic school! The culture didn't allow it, but the nuns did. They were compassionate, forward-thinking, out-of-the-box women who were respectful of the baby in her and of Joan, the young woman who made a mistake." Joan was allowed to continue her education as an unwed mother—a rare concession in the 1970s.

This was the first time Joan realized she could be an influence on others. "I registered for my senior year classes two weeks from my due date," she says. "I'll never forget the look on the new girls' faces as they walked into St. Mary's Academy and saw me. I so wanted to say to them 'This doesn't have to happen to you. Be smart.'"

At the tender age of 17, Providence stepped into Joan's life, offering her the first opportunity to learn from her mistakes and help others learn from theirs. With the support of her family, school system and boyfriend, Joan could have been an influence for others, helping them make smarter choices in their lives. But she chose not to. She simply didn't connect the pregnancy to the poor decisions she was making through her alcohol and drug abuse. She didn't understand that she needed to change.

Joan delivered her son on Sept. 1, 1974, sent him to his adoptive family and went back to complete her senior year of high school. She continued to date Tom, to party, to be the social butterfly. "She was a *rah rah*," Mara says, describing someone who was fun and impulsive, rather than rebellious.

A great practical joker, Joan once hung a sign outside her classroom window that read, "Help! We are being held hostage!" The practical joke backfired when the police showed up.

"I always had to be in the limelight," Joan says.

Along with her sense of fun came a deeply caring, compassionate side. Mara remembers Joan as someone who was friendly with everyone, took the time to ask how others were doing and was always ready with a kind word and a hello. Even with the scandal of the pregnancy, her drinking and her drug use, Joan's kindness and compassion made her popular enough to win a place in the court at both the 1974 Winter Formal and the 1975 senior prom.

"I wasn't very cliquey," Joan says with a smile.

Mara agrees, saying, "She was the same to everybody. I don't remember anybody ever talking about her. Everybody felt good about Joan. She was nice to everybody!"

Unfortunately for Joan, Providence was still trying to get her attention and had a brutal life lesson waiting for her. Tom, the teenage love of her life, died just weeks before the senior prom. High on drugs as he raced his 1966 Mustang convertible around a curve, Tom lost control, flipping the car, which ejected him and his best friend. Both died on impact.

"I remember being woken up by my mom to tell me Tom was dead," Joan says. "It was surreal—watching the news and even getting pissed at the news anchor for saying Tom lost his life on a 'joyride' at the beach."

Devastated, Joan couldn't accept Tom's death. Even after seeing his body in his coffin at the funeral home, she couldn't be convinced he had died. "I told him the joke was over, and it was time now to get up and go home."

Instead of attending her prom as a princess with her knight in shining armor, a heartbroken Joan and Tom's brother went together in Tom's memory. "It was the worst prom of my life," she says, still tearful at the memory 30 years later.

After Tom's death, Joan lost what little control she had over her drinking and drug use. It may have started as a way to be part of the in-crowd, but it became her way to drive the pain away.

"It became self-medication to get away from the pain of losing Tom and giving away the baby," Kathy says. "I think Tom's death was the tipping point that drove her into socialized alcoholism."

Joan's Life of Crime

She didn't plan on committing her first crime. It just happened. The rules at St. Mary's Academy required students to wear uniforms, but they were allowed to choose their own socks and shoes. These were status symbol for the girls, and Joan simply wanted to show off her fashion sense.

"I thought I had to keep up with the girls who had money," she says.

With six girls in private school, her parents had little money left to spend on luxuries, such as dozens of pairs of high-end shoes and fancy, frilly socks. Standing in a department store one day, Joan impulsively decided to steal a pair of socks when no one was looking. Amazed that she got away with it, Joan kept right on stealing. Soon, she had just as many fancy shoes and socks as the richest girl in school.

Although her shoplifting may have started impulsively, Joan quickly discovered the lucrative world of retail theft. She got a job as a cashier in a department store, and she graduated from shoplifting to voiding sales and pocketing cash while working the register. Surprisingly, her employers appeared oblivious to her activities. Joan was so happy and personable, it seemed impossible that she could be the one choosing to steal from them. Instead of losing her job, she consistently received promotions due to her charm and bubbly personality.

As her professional career grew, so did her repertoire of techniques. One favorite stunt involved filling boxes from the department storeroom with clothing, shipping them to her house and selling the stolen goods to unsuspecting neighbors and friends.

She was finally caught when her roommate and partner in crime was apprehended and confessed. Although the store executives asked her to refund the cost of the merchandise she had stolen, they chose not to file criminal charges. They liked Joan and couldn't accept she would be behind a plan to harm their business. Instead, they believed she had responded impulsively to an opportunity and would never do it again. Their faith in her, their willingness to look beyond the thief and at the person they knew she really was should have been a second chance to make better choices, but Joan just kept heading down the wrong path.

The strain of living as a criminal driven by alcohol and drugs changed Joan. She was no longer the friendly, confident, happy person she had once been. Her self-esteem had fallen to such a low that she believed her only value came from being seen as the impulsive, up-for-anything party girl, the hard core drinker or the successful thief. She no longer knew how to define herself.

At the same time, the *real* Joan still existed, buried deep inside. At her core, she was still the person she had once been. She was loving and kind. She wanted to make people happy. She wanted to be accepted. She wanted to love and to be loved. She just couldn't connect the dots that her poor choices were keeping her from the life she wanted. Even causing a car crash while driving drunk failed to wake her up.

"I was underage and drinking on a fake ID. One night as I was driving home from the Last Hurrah in downtown Portland, I fell asleep at the wheel and plowed into a parked car," she remembered. "I don't know how fast I was going, but my little '68 red Volkswagen convertible pushed a smaller car up a flight of stairs and almost onto the porch. Here's the kicker: I took off! I stashed my now smashed-up car at an abandoned gas station and started walking home holding a pillow over my head because it was raining. No one was hurt, but I still ran."

As she ran down the middle of the road, a police officer stopped her to ask if everything was OK. With no idea she had run from the scene of a crime, he asked a few routine questions about what she was doing out in the rain, then told her to be careful and drove away. Once again, there were no repercussions to Joan's actions.

"I wish I had gotten caught," she later admitted. "I might have changed my behavior earlier."

By 1986, Joan's life had descended into a living hell. Her drinking increased to the point that she was downing up to a half-gallon of wine a night to dull the pain of her reality. In a vain attempt to make herself feel better about her life, Joan added cocaine to the mix. Not only did choice not make her feel better, but it also led to her moving in with an abusive, drug -dealing boyfriend, who expected her to assist him in his drug-selling business. If she declined, he would beat her. "It was the worst of my relationships," she says sadly.

Using and dealing cocaine fueled her downward spiral, and her life continued to spin out of control. Still, she never got caught.

"One night, I was driving home with a half gram of cocaine that I had just bought in my purse, and I was getting ready to turn left. All of a sudden, there was a cop behind me, and he turned on his lights. I thought, 'holy crap!' but he went around me. A half gram of cocaine in those days was a *lot* of cocaine. It was bustable." For Joan, it was another close call that wasn't quite enough to make her change her ways.

At times, Joan tried to bring some normalcy into her life. She found a job working as an optician in a manufacturing lab producing eyeglasses but the job didn't last long. Her boss quickly tired of her coming to work wasted, when she bothered to show up at all, and fired her. Sitting at home with nothing to do escalated her drug and alcohol use, destroying what little self-esteem she had left.

High school friend Kathy saw Joan at their 15-year reunion in Sellwood Park in Portland and was alarmed by the changes in her childhood friend. "By the time you came to the picnic, you were really drunk," she told Joan later.

Kathy remembers talking with several other people at the reunion about the horrifying difference in Joan. "Those of us who hadn't seen her in a few years were shocked. They would say, 'Oh, what's up with Joan?'" Kathy says. "It was disappointing to me—that sweet Joan was having these issues."

Joan understood that her friends and family thought her lifestyle was destructive, but she thought they were overreacting. She knew on some level that her poor choices were responsible for her life of crime, partying and alcohol and drug abuse, but believed she had it under control. She couldn't see the cost to her relationships, her self-esteem or her future.

Waking Joan up to the problems in her life, and the opportunity to take a new path, was going to take something major.

It was going to take John Miller.

Joan Meets John

Joan had finagled herself into yet another optical lab job in 1987 when she first saw John Miller. He caught her attention when he walked by her desk with a note pinned to his shirt that read, *Because the Universe Is Expanding.*

"It was a response to questions from fellow employees about my ever-changing work hours," he laughs, saying he wore it to throw people a curve.

Soft spoken, mild mannered and with a tendency to fade into the background, John seemed an odd person to pique Joan's interest. She wasn't sure what to make of him, and he didn't seem to notice her. For the outgoing and rambunctious Joan, who demanded that everyone pay attention to her, this was unacceptable. She took his reserved nature as a personal challenge and quickly requested an introduction from a coworker. Once she learned his name, the game was on.

"Every time he came by my work station, I'd say 'Hi, John,' and wait for an answer. I got a bit of a mumble, a half smile, and he kept on walking. But that was not good enough. Every day I repeated my greeting and he gradually opened up more and more. Nothing too personal, however, he was polite and very kind. He was totally nothing like I'd come in contact with for years," she says.

Slowly but surely, through sheer persistence, Joan got John to open up. This man, who was so different from anyone she had met before, intrigued her. He was calm, cool and collected. He thought before he acted. He moved with a purpose and knew what he wanted from life. And he was completely undone by the whirlwind that was Joan.

"Joan has a tendency to kind of be going off like this, in every direction," John says, waving his arms wildly in the air. "And I'm more linear in my thinking and my direction. I also tend to take things very literally."

Their unexpected friendship grew as the months went on. Although they had little in common and had completely different personalities, they just clicked. John had no idea what kind of life Joan was living, and to her surprise Joan realized she didn't want him to know. She was enjoying this relationship. She was simply Joan; he was simply John. They were simply friends. The truth about her life came out slowly, in bits and pieces.

"I had known her for about a year or so before I became aware there was a problem in the relationship she was in," John said. "She would come to work kind of beat up—not horribly but, obviously, something had happened."

Over the next six years, as their friendship grew, John helped Joan see a different view of herself, her life and her relationships. He knew from the moment he met her that there was more to her than just an impulsive party girl. John saw the interesting, loving and downright fun person hidden underneath the facade of bad decision making, and he wanted her to see it, too. With his help, Joan began to understand that she could have value as a person. She could be someone who mattered to others.

"John was the only man I ever had a friendship with," Joan said. "Through him, I knew I was worth more."

With John's help, Joan began to realize she had other options. She didn't have to remain a drug-addicted, alcoholic criminal. She could be someone important, someone worthy of love. She could make the choice to have an entirely different life with a man who was strong enough to love her, in spite of her faults.

This was new, unnerving territory for Joan. For the first time, she realized there could be another life out there for her, if she were willing to change her ways. She could choose to leave who she was behind and become someone different. She could choose to focus on building a life with someone completely different from the men of her past—someone like John. For the first time, Joan felt hope that she could choose a better future.

After six long years Joan finally gathered up her courage, told her boyfriend she was leaving and started packing her clothes. He did not take the news well. When he started beating her once again, Joan finally called the police. "They took him away. I drove to John's house, and we've been together ever since," she said.

As she walked through the doors of John's house that night in 1991, Joan realized she had made a choice to begin a brand new life, and she vowed not to screw up. She understood that keeping John, the island of sanity in her chaotic world, meant stopping her illegal activities and drug use once and for all.

"The drugs brought out so much ugliness, so much pain," Joan says. "I didn't want that around John." She had finally found a reason to change her life.

"I'd never before met a man who accepted me for me," Joan says. "That was possibly a reason I drank like I did. I was always a girlfriend or something along those lines. I was never *just Joan* and, quite frankly, didn't know how to be. John accepted me for who I was, with all my bad faults I brought to the table. This was foreign to me, but I liked it."

Joan was optimistic about this new relationship, but she worried about meeting John's family. Would they also accept her, despite her faults? Would they think she was worthy of this wonderful man? To her surprise, his entire family welcomed her with open arms, although some of the first impressions may have been less than dignified.

John's sister, Shawn, reserved and soft spoken like her brother, didn't quite know what to make of this outgoing, boisterous woman John had fallen for. Their first meeting at a parade in downtown Portland was less than encouraging.

"What I remember is that Joan was very enthusiastic about everything," Shawn says diplomatically about that initial introduction.

"I love parades," Joan says.

"You love a lot of things, and you show it. Joan saw something that she liked in the parade, and she started doing the *coyote thing*," Shawn says, describing a tongue rolling, yelping scream Joan was known for.

Connecting this rambunctious woman with her laid back and reserved brother was a bit disconcerting for

Shawn. Unsure of what to think about the relationship after meeting Joan, Shawn told herself that for John's sake she would reserve judgment until she had a chance to get to know Joan better.

The second time they met, at Shawn's house, things didn't start out much better. John and Shawn's husband, Van, had gone into the garage, leaving the women sitting uncomfortably alone at the kitchen table.

"I was doing my nails, and Joan sat down next to me, started jabbering at me in this kooky Eastern accent and said, 'Hi, Nadine,'" Shawn says. "And I said, 'Hi, Edith.' We did that back and forth, and it just took off. It was completely out of my character."

Shawn and Joan had nothing in common and were completely different personalities, but by the time the men came back in from the garage, the two women had become fast friends. This friendship became even stronger when Shawn invited John and Joan to stay with her and Van while they were looking for a place of their own.

"While they were saving up money and looking for an apartment, they stayed in my son's old room," Shawn says.

Living so closely with John and his family forced Joan to confront her past and to determine where she wanted to go in her future. Whether she liked it or not, the time to reevaluate her life had come.

"There was so much anger," Joan recounts. She took a hard look at the way she had been living. "My drinking and drug use had nothing to do with my home life; it had nothing to do with school. It was all about my bad choices that were all coming back to bite me in the butt."

She was only beginning to realize the depth of the mistakes she had made over the years, and she was determined not to repeat them. Amazed that John and his family had accepted her, she realized she had been given a second chance. These people were willing to see her for who she was becoming rather than who she had been, and she had no intention of disappointing them.

"There is not one member of this family who has ever judged Joan's past experience," Shawn says. "We could see that core person, and that's who we related to. The Joan we had was still rough around the edges and was still dealing with a lot of repressed anger and alcohol, but the drugs were out of the picture, and what was most important for us was how she made our brother feel."

At the same time, Shawn admits that the family found Joan an odd choice for John. "Although none of us judged Joan, none of us could see what they possibly had in common," Shawn says. In the end, it didn't matter. For Shawn and the rest of the family, what mattered was that Joan made John happy.

Even with their overwhelming acceptance, fitting into this new family wasn't easy for Joan. The Millers were a quiet, reserved, intellectual family, completely unlike anyone Joan had met before. Joan had always put her social life ahead of her education, so being surrounded by these academic people often made her feel self-conscious and unprepared. Living with them presented an entirely new set of challenges.

"We were big readers, with big vocabularies, and that was hard for Joan," Shawn says. "We like to talk about things and use the vocabulary we had, and that was foreign to her. Joan sort of resented that we had what she thought of as 'higher thoughts.' She felt stupid. That was a common thread, and I'm sure that was a common thread throughout her childhood. She didn't feel good enough. She felt she was stupid. She was full of negative self-talk."

Something as simple as asking for the definition of a word made Joan feel incompetent. "She was embarrassed, because she didn't know the words," Shawn said. "She did not know how intelligent she was."

Joan feared her lack of knowledge would make John's family think less of her and somehow push him away. She worried that if she embarrassed him, he wouldn't think she was worthy of his love.

"I loved this man and wanted to impress him, and then Shawn and John would go off into these conversations, and I would think, 'Oh crap! There they go again,'" Joan says.

John and the entire Miller clan were aware of Joan's struggles and were willing to teach her about the things that interested them, if she wanted to learn. If she didn't, that was fine, too. They were happy just to have her around. Unfortunately, Joan couldn't see it that way. In Joan's experience, others wanted her to fill a role they gave her, whether that was as a drug dealer, thief, drunk cheerleader or girlfriend. She believed the only way she could be accepted was to change to fit someone else's expectations.

Being with John and his family left her at a loss. She just couldn't figure out who these people wanted her to be. It seemed the Miller family expected her to be happy with herself, and she couldn't figure out what that meant. Alternately excited and disturbed, Joan didn't even know where to start. Struggling to cope with the uncertainty of her life, she turned to the only thing that made sense: alcohol.

"I might have thought alcohol made me who I was supposed to be," Joan says. "Thinking about it now, I really did have self-esteem issues, and alcohol took them all away. I could be the *party girl,* the girl that everyone liked. And isn't that something we all want? To be liked? I actually didn't know I could be me, the real girl, and still be liked," Joan says sadly.

Shawn knew Joan believed the only way she could be accepted was if she played a part, and the part she felt most comfortable in was the center-of-attention party girl. It didn't matter if that attention was positive or negative, as long as it was attention.

"Joan had a need to make sure everyone knew she was in the room," Shawn says.

"I thought I was pretty self-confident, but I think it was the alcohol that made me think that," Joan says. "I didn't see the ugliness it created until afterward. It's like being drunk and then being sober. You think, Oh my god, I talked that loud? I danced naked?"

Once she joined the quiet Miller family, who didn't need someone to be the life of the party, Joan had a dilemma. She had gladly given up the drugs and the crime to become part of John's life, but still used alcohol to self-medicate and hide her insecurities. She desperately wanted to fit in and didn't want them to know just how much she relied on alcohol to get through the day. She started hiding small bottles of vodka around the house—in cabinets, closets, dresser drawers, wherever she could think of.

"I'd go buy little airplane bottles of vodka, because they offered a quick buzz," Joan says, "then hide them." She convinced herself that if they couldn't find her alcohol, or if they found only little bottles, they wouldn't know about her drinking problem. This, of course, fooled no one.

"Oh hell, John knew," Joan says as she remembered how ineffective her plan was. "They all knew! … I didn't know that they could hear me slurring my words."

True, the entire family knew Joan drank to excess. They just had no idea how to help. Sure, she may have been noisy, odd, sometimes out of control and always smelling of alcohol, but they liked her, so they were willing to pretend everything was okay. They didn't think of it in terms of enabling her. They believed they were being sympathetic by understanding she drank to avoid dealing with her pain. They hoped that if they just loved her enough, she would get better.

As a heavy drinker himself, John recognized that Joan had a problem, but he had no idea how to help. "This was a new relationship for all of us," John says. "What do you do? Do you take this person that you barely know and do an intervention? No. I was just trying to figure it out, what I needed to do, where I needed to go."

John, Shawn and the rest of the family were committed to keeping Joan in their lives. Just like her friends in high school, these new people saw love and kindness when they looked at Joan instead of a series of bad choices. They could see Joan's potential, even if she couldn't.

Happily Ever After

In November, 1991, Joan and John moved into an apartment in Milwaukie, Ore, and began the next chapter in their lives together. Moving in with John and committing to this relationship brought out a new side of Joan.

"In all honesty, I can say I never really got the opportunity to see and know myself until I met John. I was so busy being what I felt I needed to be at the time—to save my sanity, a relationship, or my life," she said. For the first time, she had the chance to discover who she was, how she fit into this relationship and what her future would bring, but it wasn't going to be easy. Happy as they were together, the ups and downs of Joan's emotional journey often disrupted their lives.

Even after all the years of friendship and months of living together, Joan still hid many of the stories of her past. As a result, some of her extreme reactions to normal situations completely baffled John. After living in an abusive relationship, Joan had lost the ability to communicate calmly about her emotions. Because she didn't know how to express herself, she would fly off the handle during the smallest arguments. While never violent, she could be downright mean, especially when drinking.

"If she felt she was being attacked, she would waste no time in counter-attacking," John says. "She never had an issue with any of my family members, but she and I had some dicey moments. I knew it was the alcohol. It wasn't Joan. It was the alcohol."

John knew from personal experience that alcohol could make you do things you wished you hadn't so it was easy for him to shift the blame. Sharing drinks together was their nightly routine and one they both enjoyed. But when they started working different shifts Joan would start drinking hours before he got off work. "I'd come home from work, and she was just totally screwed up," John says. "She was convinced I wouldn't know because it was vodka, and you couldn't smell it."

Finally, after one particularly trying night, John had enough. He told Joan he was tired of her drinking and the constant fighting. The next morning, after she left for work, John collected all the bottles she had been hiding around the house.

"I dumped them out and left the bottles on the counter with a note that said, 'Please Stop.' And she did stop drinking the hard stuff. She switched to beer."

Joan and John truly believed this was going to be the change they both hoped for. Neither realized that beating alcoholism meant avoiding any kind of alcohol, not just hard liquor. They pinned their hopes on the idea that if Joan drank beer like John did instead of vodka she could control her drinking. Their lives could move forward.

To her delight, John proposed to Joan on Jan. 18, 1992, at the Yaquina Head Lighthouse in Newport, Ore. Later that year, they held a simple marriage ceremony in her parents' backyard.

"My mom and I made my dress. I sewed hundreds of beads, one at a time, for embellishment," Joan said.

After the ceremony, the wedding party went to dinner at a nearby restaurant, with Joan still in her wedding dress. When they walked in, a little girl asked Joan if she could touch her.

"She thought I was a princess," Joan said. "It almost made me cry. I said I wasn't a princess, I had gotten married today and this was my wedding dress."

It was the perfect ending to a perfect day. She may have told the little girl she wasn't truly a princess, but she felt like one. Joan had turned her life around, and her reward was her *Prince Charming* and her *Happily Ever After*.

After the wedding, they purchased a home in the Gateway neighborhood of Portland. Not long after they moved in, Joan walked into work and sitting next to her desk was a small dog wearing a big red bow. The note attached to the bow said, "I want to live in a little yellow house with a man named John and a woman named Joan." A gift from her friend, Josie, the puppy named Wile E. would be a treasured family member for the next 12 years.

Ecstatic that her life was finally coming together, Joan felt she had chosen the right path. She convinced herself that because she had stopped drinking vodka and hiding the bottles and only drank beer, she had reached the end of her struggle with alcohol. But that wasn't true.

John and Joan simply didn't see the bigger problem. After all, lots of couples used beer in the evening as a way to connect and unwind. Why couldn't they? It wasn't long before they had developed a nightly routine of getting off work, picking up a short case of beer and finishing it off before bed. Because they were happy they believed this ritual was a normal part of married life.

And they *were* happy. When Joan thought about her earlier life, this new life seemed miraculous. They had their home, steady jobs and loving friends and family. Joan didn't think her life could get any better. She and John even started an Amway business that they hoped would teach them business and public speaking skills and help them become successful entrepreneurs.

"Joan became very directed and focused," Shawn says. That exuberant cheerleader nature made her a natural for sharing things she believed in, and the Amway business model gave her the opportunity to practice communicating. As she became more comfortable speaking in public, Joan found talents she didn't know she possessed. Whether talking one-on-one or up in front of a crowd, she was sharing her vision and having a ball.

Joan's dreams were finally coming true. She had no idea it would only last for seven years.

The Hostage

After her release from McKay-Dee Hospital, Joan flew home to Portland and began the lengthy recovery process to regain a semblance of life. To Joan, recovery meant a bewildering, painful and frustrating journey that would last for years. To Joan's family, excited that she was alive and awake, recovery meant accepting that the process may be much longer and more difficult than they ever imagined.

Joan's journey began on June 23, 1999, at the Rehabilitation Institute of Oregon (RIO) at Legacy's Good Samaritan Medical Center in Portland. RIO was an inpatient treatment facility that specialized in spinal cord and brain injuries, including Traumatic Brain Injuries (TBIs), such as Joan's. Here, Joan would spend the next 30 days working with a team comprising of doctors, nurses, therapists, nutritionists, spiritual support and even horticultural therapists. The goal was to help Joan gain enough independence to leave the hospital and begin outpatient therapy.

When Joan first arrived at RIO, the staff performed a complete assessment to determine her capabilities. What was her baseline? Where would they need to start? The results were not encouraging. Although the members of both her and John's families believed they were ready for the results, the evaluation still came as a blow.

"We didn't have any idea of the scope of the damage, even though it was explained to us. Seeing it played out during the assessment was a completely different thing," Shawn says. They knew and accepted that Joan needed to relearn everything from how to swallow and how to walk in a straight line to how to speak clearly. They were less prepared for the intellectual and emotional damage.

The worst moment came during the evaluation of Joan's ability to read. The doctor placed a sheet of paper on the table in front of her and asked Joan to read the words written on it. To Shawn's dismay, Joan bent over and put her eye on the table instead of picking up the paper and bringing it to eye level.

"It took that for Johnny and me to recognize just how damaged her vision was. It was horrible, I have to say," Shawn recalls.

Soon after came a test of her writing ability, which went no better. Joan hadn't forgotten how to write, but she struggled with getting her hands and fingers to hold the pencil to form the words, which made sense based on the seriousness of her injuries. What shocked John the most was realizing Joan thought her writing looked completely normal.

"As far as she was concerned, she was probably writing just fine," John says. "But her writing was atrocious. It was like a kid just learning to write—if that good; it was just a scrawl that made no sense at all."

Dr. Welling and his team had tried to explain the extent of her injuries, but no one in either family was prepared for the reality. Sure, when she tried to swallow water it dribbled out of her mouth. Sure, she couldn't sit down without help. Sure, she wobbled when she walked. They understood those were the physical results of a terrible car crash. Recovery would be difficult, but possible.

"Unbelievably," Shawn says, "We still believed it would be six months, and she would be fine."

Now, they were seeing another layer to the reality of her injury. Her loss of the ability to read and write, combined with her belief that this was normal, was terrifying. This was more than damage to her body. This meant damage to her mind. How could this be fixed? They knew, and were grateful, that Joan had already beaten the odds by being alive. Now, they wanted to know if the RIO staff could repair her ability to think and reason. Could they bring their Joan back to them?

As traumatized as they were by the test results, they still had hope that treatment in RIO would help save Joan. After all, this was one of the top five rehabilitation centers in the nation. If anyone could help Joan, it would be the experienced staff at this facility. They were all confident Joan was in the best of hands. They just had to get Joan to cooperate.

Joan had a completely different take on the entire situation. In her mind, this move to RIO involved a conspiracy to keep her held as a prisoner. She didn't believe she was in a rehabilitation facility trying to recover from a car crash and brain injury. Instead, she believed she was a prisoner at St. Mary's Academy, her old high school. It made perfect sense to Joan. This was a red, three-story building, and St. Mary's was a red, three-story building. It was obvious: She was at St. Mary's, and nothing anyone said was going to change her mind.

"We would tell her where she was, and she wouldn't believe us," Shawn says. "She was right, and she didn't want to argue with us."

Trying to reason with her was useless. When those around her pointed out the hospital rooms or the medical equipment, she simply discounted what they said. Even trying specific arguments, such as asking how she explained the medical staff wandering the halls and in and out of her room, didn't help. She knew who they were. They were her captors, unknown people using her for nefarious purposes to earn a paycheck.

"I was firmly convinced that the only reason I was in this facility was because those people needed a job," she says.

Joan even believed the members of her own family were in on the scheme. It didn't matter to her that John was at her side all day, every day, or that someone from her family or John's was always nearby. The fact that they eventually left was all the proof she needed that they were all in cahoots.

"I knew for a fact the doctors had sold them on some bill of goods," Joan says. "That's why they never stayed very long. They told me it was so I could rest, that they didn't want to tire me out, that rest was the single most important thing for me now. What a crock! They had to leave so the staff could play more games with me."

To add insult to injury, the staff infuriated Joan when they insisted she was 42 years old. In her mind, that was simply not possible. In the hours between leaving Utah and arriving in Portland, Joan had lost an entire decade. She was only 34, and no one could convince her otherwise.

The Enemy

According to Certified Occupational Therapist Michelle Moffett, Joan's arch-nemesis during her stay at RIO, these were normal reactions. Damage to the brain often results in the lack of "insight," the ability of people to understand what is happening around them.

"It's very common when people have a brain injury," Michelle says. "Unless your brain recognizes that you have a problem, you can't get better."

For occupational therapists like Michelle, this lack of insight presents a much bigger challenge than the physical injury itself. "You have to make them understand that they have a traumatic brain injury," she explains.

Michelle compares a brain injury to a computer that is offline. The swelling and damage to the tissue prevents the transfer of information from Point A to Point B, and the system crashes. The hope is that as time goes on, the swelling goes down, and the brain comes back online. If the swelling remains, the damaged part of the brain needs to be rewired, so it can go around the blockage. This meant intensive, costly and, often, painful treatment to relearn how to function as a person.

"We can't always rewire properly," Michelle says. "Joan has had a great recovery, and she has worked hard at it, but not everybody gets that."

Recovery meant first helping Joan understand that she had a brain injury. Denial that there was anything wrong was one of the most difficult things Joan, like most brain injury patients, faced. Michelle believed that this kind of denial might have been a way for the brain to protect itself, or the personality, from the magnitude of the injury. Instead of facing all that had been lost, the brain looked for ways to block some of it out. But until Joan's brain accepted there was a problem, her body simply couldn't heal. And she needed help healing. While most of the attention was focused on her brain injury, Joan also had a cracked pelvis and nerve damage to her shoulder and arm. She just didn't know it, because her brain wouldn't let her see the damage.

"The brain is the master and commander of the ship," Michelle says. "If the brain is telling you there's not a problem, how can you get better?"

Joan became increasingly frustrated by Michelle's insistence on this idea that she had a brain injury and additional injuries that she couldn't see. Either she was hurt, or she wasn't. If she was, Joan was sure she would have been the first to know. Joan was convinced Michelle was just making it up.

"Hearing about that was hearing gibberish," Joan says. "Once again, if I couldn't see it, it wasn't there."

Along with helping Joan understand how badly she was hurt, Michelle also needed to evaluate what Joan would need to relearn to regain her independence.

"It begins with the basics," Michelle says. Each morning, when Michelle came into Joan's room, she evaluated what Joan could do that day. Could she stand? Could she bathe? Shower? Use the toilet? In the morning Joan could remember how to walk, then she would forget how to put one foot in front of the other in the afternoon. Some days she could drink a glass of milk at breakfast, and other days she dribbled it down the front of her gown. Michelle needed to test Joan over and over to find what she could and couldn't do.

"Did that piss me off?" Joan later asked Michelle.

"You didn't like it," Michelle replies diplomatically. Then she laughs, "Let's just say you weren't a willing participant."

"It's because I knew I could do it, and you just needed a job," Joan says.

In addition to evaluating Joan physically, Michelle tested Joan's cognitive skills each day. Could she remember a task she had learned the day before? Solve a simple problem? Memory challenges after a brain injury are common, and Joan proved no exception.

"She had a pretty significant brain injury," Michelle says candidly. "Her memory was toast."

At 8:00 a.m., she could remember her husband's name and then forget it three hours later. She often forgot what she was doing or what she meant to say and then forget she had forgotten. It was a vicious cycle

To help improve Joan's thinking and memory skills and raise Joan's awareness of her injuries Michelle would wander in and out of her room throughout the day and perform a series of memory exercises. One of Michelle's favorite techniques involved walking through the door with her hand over her name tag and asking Joan, "What's my name?"

If Joan couldn't answer, Michelle gave her clues.

"You don't give the brain all the information," she explains, "because it gets lazy."

Instead, she would tell Joan that her name started with an M. If that did not work, she would give bigger clues, like offering a choice between Michelle, Marie or Margaret. If Joan still could not remember, she would reintroduce herself as Michelle.

This process did not make Joan happy. Even after she understood the exercise had a purpose, Joan resented Michelle's insistence on repeating it.

"That name tag thing," Joan snickers. "That was directed at me, and she was doing it just to piss me off. She would come into the room with her hand over her name tag and ask me what her name was, and I would say, 'I don't know, why don't you move your hand?' It got to the point where she would walk in the room, and I would immediately say, 'Move your damn hand!'"

Michelle refers to these interactions as somewhat tedious and frustrating for both the patient and the therapist. Joan put it more bluntly. "I hated her!" she says. "She would piss me off so bad I'd have to prove her wrong. I'd have to get her to shut up and get out of my room."

Finding the balance between pushing Joan to succeed and upsetting her to the point that she shut down required that Michelle constantly find new ways to encourage and engage Joan. Passionate about her work, Michelle has an entire bag of tricks to help her patients move forward, but they don't always make it easy. Part of her job as a therapist requires figuring out how to reach each unique person without a blueprint of what emotionally motivates them, and Joan was no different.

"It all depends on where the injury was, their personality, their support system, their life history, everything," she explains. "What can I do? Can I beg, borrow, steal? Do I demand? How do I fit into her personality so that she is on board with the therapy?"

Once Michelle learned that Joan believed she was being held captive by people who needed jobs, she quickly used that theory to get Joan to play along. She believed she could gain Joan's cooperation by convincing her that the faster she got through the process, the faster she could leave. It worked, to a point.

Joan might have been willing to jump through Michelle's hoops to escape, but that didn't mean she bought into the story her captors were telling. No matter how reasonable Michelle's answers were, Joan could always find another version of reality. One common situation revolved around Joan falling over if she tried to walk without help.

When Michelle tried patiently, once again, to explain to Joan that she had an injury she was unaware of, Joan cried foul. Joan, who didn't realize she had a leg injury, had a better explanation: One of the people helping her must have pushed her. The only other option would have been Michelle's and Joan wasn't buying that. When Michelle took the opposite tack and challenged her to explain why she wobbled, Joan refused to answer.

"Of course I knew how to walk," Joan insists. "You get out of bed and do it!"

After almost falling several more times, Joan finally acknowledged she was having a problem walking. She might not have been ready to admit that a problem existed between her legs and her brain, but she would allow the possibility that something wasn't working as it should. Michelle quickly jumped on the opportunity, setting up situations that would encourage Joan to practice getting around. She even used John as bait.

"When I was learning how to walk again, transitioning out of the wheelchair into a walker, I challenged myself to walk to the bathroom without anyone's assistance," Joan says.

She told herself that if she could do that, she could walk across the room unaided and kiss her husband. It took years before Joan gave credit to Michelle for putting the idea into her head in the first place, referring to the plan as yet another one of Michelle's sneak attacks to get her to cooperate.

Joan also slowly figured out that she had a skull fracture. "My head was bandaged, so I realized my head got hurt," Joan says. Still, still couldn't connect the bandage to a brain injury. That concept remained one of Michelle's insane ideas.

"You thought everyone else was crazy," Michelle said to Joan later. "You thought we were all screwed up and should just let you go home. We were crazy, and you were fine."

Joan firmly held to her conspiracy theory and her belief that she was nothing more than a means to a paycheck for the people who wandered in and out of her room. Not only were they there simply to make her miserable, they were getting paid for it. It was unbelievably unfair.

"It seemed that just as soon as I got back to my room, along came someone who forced me to do something I didn't want to do, or didn't think I needed to do. They never left me alone!" she says. "Any of the brain work was something they did to me to either keep me humble or piss me off. The latter to be sure. I was a sort of guinea pig for all these students who wanted to be in the medical field so they had to find them something to do."

Joan knew that the people around her, including Michelle, the doctors, John, her sisters and all the other members of both families wanted her to accept she had been badly injured. They believed that something had happened that had changed her, something that left her less than she had been before. Even worse, they wanted her to believe it also. No matter how they pushed and insisted, Joan couldn't agree.

Joan knew she was the same person she had always been. Her feet had never worked quite right and her eyes had always pointed the wrong way. She always had forgotten her husband's name and written in a scrawl that looked like it belonged to a 2-year-old. Regardless of what everyone around her said, Joan knew there was nothing wrong with her. That meant it had to be those around her, those holding her hostage, who had the problem.

Learning to Make Toast

There was some truth to Joan's hostage claims. Although her conspiracy theories were untrue, Joan might have had a reason to think they were holding her against her will. Keeping patients safe is a huge challenge for the RIO staff, involving constant supervision, locked doors on the rehabilitation floor and wheelchairs with seatbelts. "It's all about safety," Michelle says. The concepts of thinking before acting and understanding that actions have consequences are simply beyond the grasp of many with a traumatic brain injury. Just like Joan.

The staff at RIO had to be constantly on guard because Joan's brain was physically so fragile that simply hitting her head after falling out of her wheelchair could have killed her.

"This is why we restrain patients," Michelle says. "They've had a brain injury. They cannot have another one. And they are unpredictable. They would say, 'I swear to God I won't get up,' and five minutes later, I would find them on the floor. You ask them what they were doing, and they say, 'I don't know. I had to go to the bathroom.'"

This lack of freedom can be extremely frustrating for the patients who believe they are fine. When Michelle reminds Joan that she too had been restrained in a wheelchair with a safety belt at the beginning of her recovery to keep her from running away, Joan flatly denies it.

Then, in the same breath, she reluctantly admits, "I would think nothing about running into the street."

Because of this impulsiveness, combined with a lack of insight and no understanding about danger, all of Joan's exercises had to include lessons in safety. It was the simple things that most people take for granted. Don't touch a burner on the stove. Don't put a knife in the toaster. Don't run in front of cars when crossing the street.

Joan couldn't access her memories of how to do the things she knew should be easy, which reinforced her belief that every task Michelle and the team at RIO planned came from a desire to show her incompetence. "I felt like she was picking on me, like she was singling me out," Joan says.

This is a common reaction for those with brain injuries. "Most people take it as an IQ thing," Michelle says: "'I could do this before, and now I can't; I'm stupid.'"

Brain injury survivors often get overwhelmed by the shuffle from physical therapy, occupational therapy and memory work required just to recover the skills needed for the basics of living. Adding to their frustration is the need to accept and navigate this strange new world they find themselves in.

As Joan progressed, Michelle added cognitive therapy exercises to help her relearn basic problem solving. Designed to continue the rebooting of her brain, these exercises used movement, sight, touch and memory to help Joan remember how to deal with what she would find outside the safety of RIO.

It began with simple things like how to use a fork or drink from a glass, how to hook a bra clasp, how to remember socks go on before shoes and how to catch a ball. Once she showed she could do these things, she progressed to more abstract tasks, such as building a tower of blocks, writing her name and putting together a puzzle.

Michelle explained that these exercises showed how one action led to another, so Joan could see the bigger picture. But Joan saw it as yet another level of insult.

"They gave me popsicle sticks to make houses," she says. She was infuriated at being asked to do the same things children do in kindergarten. At the same time, realizing these simple tasks were challenging confused her. Somewhere in her mind, she knew she should be able to glue popsicle sticks together, but she couldn't make it happen. Instead of grabbing a handful of sticks and making a house, she had to think about each tiny step. How many popsicle sticks should she glue at one time? How much glue did she need? Where does the popsicle stick go if it needs to be the roof? Shocked, she realized she had to stop and think about every step.

As she progressed from what she called *the kindergarten stuff*, the staff added more complicated tasks. Her next assignments were in the RIO training kitchen for classes in the practical life skills she would need when she went home. Designed as a way to help patients make the transition to home from the safety of RIO, the training kitchen included an oven, refrigerator, coffee maker, toaster and dishwasher.

Staff used this setup to teach Joan more practical lessons in problem-solving and safety. *Lessons like: When a stove burner turns red, it is hot. Do not touch it.*

Not surprisingly, Joan found the idea that she had to attend a class in correctly moving around a kitchen irritating and insulting.

For someone with a brain injury, something as simple as making a piece of toast can be an exercise in aggravation. Before the crash, Joan walked into her kitchen at 5 a.m., popped a piece of bread in a toaster and grabbed the butter, all while starting the coffee. She didn't realize that now she had to learn to stop, think out each step and plan each action before she moved.

"They told me they were going to teach me how to make toast! How stupid do they think I am that I have to learn to make toast?" Joan grumbled. "I was so angry. It was so humiliating that I would fake a need to go the bathroom just to waste time, hoping the class would be over by the time I got back. It worked once. Then it was 'Joan go to the bathroom, and then we will learn to make toast.'"

Even as the staff insisted they were teaching her skills she needed to function around the house, Joan refused to believe it.

"What they're really doing is messing with the mentals. Making toast isn't something you think about. It is something you do, like walking, talking or breathing. It is common knowledge. I figured I should know what a toaster is. It's a toaster! It's like your shoes: You have a right shoe and a left shoe, and you know what they are."

Then she walked into the training kitchen and couldn't find the toaster. There were multiple appliances on the counter, but none of them looked quite right. Undeterred from her conspiracy mindset, Joan blamed her inability to figure out what piece of equipment she needed on a vindictive staff intentionally hiding it from her to make her look stupid. Once the therapist helped her figure out that the toaster sat on the counter directly in front of her, she realized she had no idea how to use it. Suddenly, something as simple as making breakfast became a multi-step process that defeated her repeatedly.

1. *Find the toaster.*

    "I had no idea the toaster was the shiny square box with the holes on top. I told them I couldn't find it, and I thought it was their fault because there wasn't even one in the kitchen. They pointed it out to me, and I thought, 'Oh! Yeah, OK.'"

2. *Open the bread bag.*

    "How do I get into the bag? What do I do to open this thing in front of me? How do I untwist the twisty thing? I was getting more and more frustrated, because I knew it was something I should know. I knew the word *bread*, but I couldn't associate it with this 'stuff' in the bag. I finally pulled out a piece of the white stuff that was inside the bag, assuming that was what they meant by *bread*."

3. *Get the bread out of the bag.*

    "I knew I had seen the stuff before, because I recognized the shape, but I couldn't figure out what to do with it. I just didn't understand this *bread* thing. I didn't know it was something that I could eat. I knew this kind of white stuff was usually around in our house, but for all I knew, it could have been a bar of soap. I knew I should know what to do with it. And I didn't."

4. *Put the bread in the toaster, and push it down.*

    "How? Do you mean those slots on the top of the silver box? I put the stuff in the slot and pushed on it. The stuff squished. It wouldn't go down. I looked at that therapist and said, 'It's bending! It's not working! Tell me!' They told me to take my hand off the bread and slide the bar down on the side of the toaster. That will make the bread go down, and when it was done it would pop up. That was how it toasts.' They also said, 'Don't touch it when it comes up because it will be hot! Things coming out of a toaster are hot. You have to let it cool down.'"

5. *Take the toast out of the toaster.*

    "They asked me if I saw how the color changed, and I said, 'No.' I wasn't able to hang onto the idea that the stuff from the bag would change after it came out of the toaster. They had to show me a piece of white bread so I could compare it to the brown toast. Once we were done making toast a couple times, I was so tired I went back to my room and went to bed."

The confusion that came from needing to plan each step of anything she wanted to do was overwhelming. Putting together a puzzle, turning on the oven or making a piece of toast, it should have been easy. Why wasn't it? Sometimes, the sense of failing in a world she couldn't understand was just too much. Even making a bed became an exercise in frustration.

"Once again I thought it would be easy, 'cause anybody can make a bed," she says. "And once again I was wrong."

Then there was the day her therapist told her they were going to go outside into the parking lot and practice getting into a car, and Joan almost went into orbit.

"This is when I thought they really flipped their lids," Joan says. "The fact that I had to get into a car that wasn't going anywhere was absolutely absurd!"

For Joan, this was yet another example of the staff's need to find humiliating things for her to do to save their own jobs. These exercises could not have been actually prescribed by her doctor.

"There was no way any doctor would have wanted them to be doing that kind of nonsense," she says. "Who would have ever thought of such a stupid thing to waste my time doing—getting in and out of a car? C'mon, this is a hospital. Act like you know what's going on! I wanted to say, 'Let's get back to the work of fixing my body. Stop with these stupid games you like playing!'"

Then she stepped out into the parking lot and realized she wasn't sure how to open the car door, much less how to maneuver into the seatbelt.

The challenges seemed never ending. "I had to relearn how to brush my hair and brush my teeth," Joan says, "along with learning to turn on the oven and tie my own shoes." It became a constant struggle to feel like a person of value instead of someone broken.

To combat the sense of failure, Joan desperately held on to her belief that the reason she couldn't remember how to do things somehow connected directly to the conspiracy theory that "these people" needed jobs. "I was just helping people out who were learning," she repeated to anyone who would listen.

No matter how hard she tried to fight their version of reality, eventually the staff wore her down. Joan finally accepted that the only way to escape was to make more of an effort to cooperate and complete the tasks they gave her—things like following the steps involved in making toast or getting into a car. Still believing she was a prisoner, she realized the only way to gain her freedom was to make them believe she had given in to their unreasonable demands.

Finding Peace in the Garden

While Joan painstakingly worked to learn how to function at a basic level and navigate the world outside, she also needed to plan for her future. Her recovery would be successful only if it included all aspects of her life, not just the damage to her brain and body.

"Some people with a TBI lose the skills to care for themselves, but most are impaired to some level," says Teresia Hazen, coordinator of the Therapeutic Gardens for Legacy Health, where RIO is based. "Patients may not remember how to do something or may not remember how to do all the steps or forget to follow the steps. But rehabilitation cannot be just about work, work, work. Life becomes so full of going to the doctor and following medical requirements that patients forget to take care of the whole person."

Teresia believes that rehabilitation has to be about more than building physical and thinking abilities. Teresia's program, one of the first to include leisure and recreational training, provides a way to help patients find their place in their new world by repairing emotional competence.

The Therapeutic Garden provided a kind of escape from the tough work of rehabilitation, and it was an escape Joan desperately needed.

In the garden, Joan found an environment that stimulated her senses while providing practical skill-building exercises in a peaceful environment. Instead of white walls, stainless steel equipment and hospital beds, the garden surrounded her with fresh air, flowering plants and fountains.

Even before Joan was fully aware of her surroundings, her doctor had cleared her for short visits to the garden. Strangely, Joan had no memories of this until she sat in on an interview with Teresia 10 years later. Suddenly she looked up and said, "I remember that! I remember thinking it was nice to get out of my room, and it was so pretty out there."

As part of Joan's therapy program, Teresia created a task-based learning system that helped her work on focus and motor control using physical movements, cognitive exercises and problem-solving skills.

"It all relates to safety, judgment, problem solving, sequencing and planning," Teresia says. "Education, education, education. What is the next little step, then the next little step ... and build on success."

The garden gave Joan's therapists a different environment to practice her skills. Inside her room, the therapist had her practice picking up a hairbrush to build hand and eye coordination. In the garden, the task was to gently touch a flower without crushing it. Inside her hospital room, she worked on relearning how to sit in a chair. In the garden, she practiced sitting on a bench.

Even when surrounded by the beauty of the garden, these routine exercises could still be devastating for Joan. Sitting down should have been something she remembered how to do. Instead, her therapist had to guide her through the steps of walking up to the seat, turning around, touching the back of her knees to the bench and then sitting down with a straight back. In the garden, at least, her anger and frustration had the benefit of fresh air and flowers.

If the weather was too dreary to go outside, Joan participated in the indoor gardening program in the activity room. "It is a way to bring something interesting into the patient's world," Teresia says. Just like in the training kitchen, Joan's tasks became more complex as she progressed. Instead of simply working on coordinating hand and eye to reach out and touch a leaf, she was asked to pluck a flower off the plant.

Once she could do that, she advanced to filling a pot with dirt and setting the plant inside it. By relearning the concept of progression, Joan began to understand how every action meant something and led to another action. This type of treatment program also helped Joan build the organizational and coping strategies she would need as she entered the next stage of treatment.

According to Teresia, Joan's recovery process would be made up of three distinct parts. First, there was RIO, where Joan's health stabilized, she learned about basic safety, and she started to relearn essential skills. Then Joan would head home and attend outpatient rehabilitation, including more physical and cognitive therapy. If her rehabilitation was successful, Joan would rejoin society as a fully functioning person with a brain injury, rather than as a brain-injured person.

To prepare emotionally for moving to the next level, Teresia taught Joan to focus on using her time in recreation therapy to focus less on what had been lost from her old life and more on where she could go in her new one. She worked with both Joan and John to discover what Joan's background had been and what leisure activities she used to enjoy. By combining the past and present, Teresia helped Joan find the balance between what she loved to do and what she could do. She then helped Joan create a plan to connect her current physical and mental condition with the things she wanted to do.

Teresia based her philosophy on the idea that people with brain injuries are still growing; they may be growing differently, but they are not growing less. She used the lessons in her garden sessions to show Joan that a brain injury did not stop forward momentum; it just changed how she moved forward. "People reinvent themselves all the time," Teresia told Joan. "RIO just helps them."

This approach helped Joan begin to understand she wasn't that different from others, that growing and learning are normal parts of everyone's life. Instead of focusing on recovery, Teresia put Joan on the path of striving to improve, using the mantra: "After a TBI you don't get your life back; you get a brand new life."

As the garden's soothing atmosphere allowed her to focus on the person she saw in the mirror each day, her need to hang on to her conspiracy theory began to decrease. Joan's work with Teresia showed her that although success was not guaranteed, an escape was coming. Eventually, Joan would have the skills she needed to be discharged from RIO.

The RIO staff had helped Joan regain her dignity. They had taught her to walk and talk, how to swallow and how to be safe. They had set her on the road toward understanding she might have a problem, even though she remained unconvinced. Now it would be up to her. Joan had come through her month at RIO physically stabilized and with the most basic skills she needed to start her new life. It was time to leave RIO and go home, where she would continue the work to become the *New Joan*.

Coming Home

For Michelle, watching Joan leave RIO was bittersweet. Although thrilled that Joan had accomplished so much, she questioned if she could survive outside the safety of RIO. "Their [people with a TBI] lives are impacted forever," Michelle says. "It's not like they come to RIO, get fixed and carry on. For most people with brain injuries, it's a forever deal."

For Michelle, the reality that insurance companies only allow 30 days in a treatment facility, such as RIO, is incredibly frustrating.

"Insurance says if you can walk 100 feet with a walker, you are better. You don't know your name, you can't sign a check, you can't add, but they will discharge you from therapy 'cause you can walk," she says. "People leave RIO, and I don't sleep. I think, oh my God how are those people going to manage? What is going to happen to them?"

Michelle also had concerns about the ability of Joan's family to provide the round-the-clock care she would need once she got home. Joan had survived and learned some basic skills, but she was still a mess. Her thoughts were confused, her balance nonexistent, she suffered from constant double vision, and she still had significant physical injuries. Even more frightening, her grasp of reality was still shaky. She may be letting go of her conspiracy theory but that didn't mean she bought into the idea that she was the one with a problem.

Joan left RIO believing she was fine, other than a few physical injuries. This idea that she needed constant monitoring so she didn't accidentally hurt herself was inconceivable. Michelle knew it would be up to Joan's family to protect her from herself, and she worried they still didn't understand the magnitude of Joan's injuries.

Michelle knew the steep learning curve the family would face as they took over caring for Joan's physical injuries, but she had faith they would figure it out. Techniques for changing bandages and helping Joan safely move from one part of a room to another were easy to teach. Helping them accept the changes in Joan's personality, on the other hand, was going to be more challenging.

Brain injuries can often exacerbate personality traits that were already there, which can explain how someone cranky by nature turns violently aggressive or how a generally unhappy person suddenly becomes profoundly depressed. For Joan, her cheerleader nature was enhanced. Before, she had been talkative and energetic, always up for a challenge and often careless in her decision making. Now, she tended toward being dangerously impulsive, but her family struggled to see the difference.

John and Shawn didn't see any changes in her behavior and argued with the doctors who said Joan had changed. They, along with the rest of the family, insisted she behaved just like she always had. This made it difficult for the RIO staff to convince them of the potential problems they would face once they brought Joan home.

The staff tried to explain that Joan simply didn't understand that actions had consequences, and without that understanding there could be no impulse control. Before, Joan would have run to the store without a grocery list. Now, she was apt to run into traffic without looking for cars. Because she no longer knew how to stop and think about the next step, she couldn't be trusted. To keep her safe, those around her had to be constantly one step ahead of her. They had to think in terms of *What will Joan do next?*, and they needed to be ready to react. Tragically, this meant they had to understand that this constant vigilance was their new normal.

Along with the patients, many families are unprepared for the reality that recovering from a brain injury requires a complete lifestyle change, according to Teresia.

"We need to give people new tools," she says.

But these tools would only work if they could get the family members to accept the seriousness of Joan's injury—and that was not going to be easy.

"It's a defense mechanism," Michelle explains the denial she faced when talking with Joan and John's family members. "It's devastating."

Devastating or not, the staff at RIO had to get Joan, John and the rest of both families on board with understanding her differences, because a mistake at this point could cost Joan her life. She simply couldn't risk another brain injury. Something as simple as hitting her head on a shower door or banging it into a door frame while falling from her walker could have completely derailed Joan's recovery.

"The person you are today would be gone," Michelle told Joan. "After a brain injury the elevator never goes all the way to the top. It may go 99%, but it will never go all the way up. Then you go and take a significant bump to the head and you're at 75, then another one and you're at 50."

It was overwhelming. For John and the families bringing Joan home required that they process all the information about Joan's injury, learn how to care for her in the future and accept the changes in her personality, learn when to help her, when *not* to help her and how to continue challenging her to move forward. All this while working jobs of their own, taking care of their own families and going about their daily lives.

At the same time, Michelle and Teresia knew the only way Joan would succeed was with the support of those around her. Luckily, Joan's support system was amazing, one that Michelle and many others credit as the main reason for Joan's remarkable recovery.

Even with all the support, it wasn't easy. John admits he felt a mixed reaction when they told him the time had come to take Joan home. He didn't realize how completely unprepared he was for what would happen next.

"I had no idea still how severe her injuries were. My leg was still in a cast when I called my boss and talked to him about what was going on. He asked me how long I was going to be off, and I told him two weeks." John says. "I was happy to have her home."

Although the staff at RIO had tried to prepare them, there were no specifics for how to care for Joan. "I don't remember anyone in particular saying, 'Watch for this or that,'" Shawn says.

Instead, they learned by trial and error. In 1999, brain injuries were still fairly unknown in the mainstream. These were the days before the daily media coverage of high-profile incidents, such as the Gabrielle Gifford shooting. The National Football League hadn't yet settled with players over concussion-related injuries. The military hadn't yet acknowledged the effects of brain damage from IED devices.

Caring for someone with a brain injury at home was basically unknown territory. As the reality set in, John accepted that he wouldn't be able to leave Joan alone for the foreseeable future. His next phone call to his boss changed his time off from two weeks to six months.

Saying he was overwhelmed would be an understatement. John, who had no medical training, brought home a wife who had barely survived a major car crash only six weeks earlier. When asked how he came to terms with taking on sole responsibility for her, he says, "You just do it. You take it moment by moment and deal with it. That's all you can do."

John knew his Joan was still in there somewhere, even if she didn't look or act like his wife anymore. The right side of her face didn't work the way it should, so her right eyebrow never moved. Her head was shaved bald except for one little wisp at the back of her neck. Her eyes pointed in different directions, and her skull had a huge concave depression. She couldn't stand without help because of her unstable balance. She wobbled when she walked, and she had to wear a helmet to protect her soft spot.

"It was a very bizarre, unsettling appearance," John says.

To add to the challenge, he never knew when she would lose track of reality. On the day he brought her home, Joan turned to him and asked, "Why are we at Rita's?" She had no memory of this house, the one she and John had lived in for five years. Instead, she wondered why he had brought her to her sister's house.

Joan explains, "I thought we were at Rita's because of the windows and blinds and where the couch was. Rita's house didn't look anything like our house, and the furniture wasn't at all like ours or anything. But the windows and blinds convinced me we were there."

Even after John finally convinced Joan that they were in their house, she continued to drift into alternate realities. She insisted on looking for a nonexistent cat they had never owned and completely forgot her dog, Wile E. She often lost her way walking from one room to another in their two-bedroom home. After one three-day medical follow-up at Good Samaritan, she came up with a story that she had spent the weekend at a friend's house watching TV in her basement.

For John, this constant occurrence was unnerving. "She would be talking to someone about something that happened, and I would be sitting there thinking it didn't happen," he says. "She didn't remember things accurately, so her brain filled in the blanks."

In addition to her flights of fancy, Joan's short-term memory loss proved to be a constant problem. Sometimes she would lose five minutes, and sometimes it was three days. She would ask Shawn for a glass of water, forget she had asked when Shawn handed it to her, and then become frustrated because she had forgotten. She would find herself standing in the kitchen crying because she didn't remember why she had left the living room, or walk into the living room with an empty plate, then get upset she was still hungry and couldn't remember where her lunch had gone.

Physically, Joan wasn't doing much better. Even something as simple as taking a shower turned into a logistical nightmare. Without the balance necessary to stand in the shower, someone needed to be right beside her every time she bathed to hold her still. Because the damage to her arm meant she still couldn't lift her arm over her head, she also needed help washing her body and hair. It was a humiliating experience.

Just getting to the bathroom in the first place meant conquering a whole new series of challenges. Her double vision meant tripping over chairs, because she couldn't figure out which one was real and which was the ghost, or missing the opening from one room to another. Navigating her own house required constant guidance and correction from others, which of course, Joan felt demeaning.

Even worse, the staff at RIO insisted she use a walker whenever she got up, even if it was only going from one room to another.

"I hated that thing!" she says. "Because I was still having a hard time navigating corners and had no spatial context, I'd run the stupid thing into the walls or door jambs. Then of course I'd come to a screeching halt, and I'd get jostled. Walking with it on the sidewalk was like running a jackhammer. Not the smoothest thing around. I was outside one day when it jammed up into my flower bed, and I was fed up so I tossed it. I remember saying, 'I'll have to do this on my own; that damn thing is only getting in the way.'"

Because of her refusal to use the walker, her therapists agreed to try to transition her to using a cane to help with her balance. For stubborn Joan, that was also less than successful.

"What a joke! What a dangerous joke," she says. "I'd forget to keep the cane to my side while I walked and inevitably trip over it. I would put it right in front of me or in front of the foot that I was going to use to take a step, and *whoops!* I caught myself too many times almost hitting the wall, so the cane went bye-bye really quickly."

Much of her resistance to cooperate with instructions came from still not comprehending she had a brain injury. As she saw it, she had finally managed to convince the staff at RIO that she was fine and ready to move to outpatient therapy. She had played along with all of their games and finally found her chance to escape. She was free.

Or so she thought. Much to her surprise, she found she simply had swapped the prison guards at RIO for one who lived in her own home. Joan may have liked John better than she liked Michelle, but she wasn't any happier with the insistence that she still needed a babysitter. Dismayed, Joan suddenly realized that not only was the conspiracy continuing, but also that John was an active part of it.

Although it was a constant struggle to keep Joan safe and secure, John was fortunate. He didn't have to do it alone. "Johnny never asked for help," Shawn says, but that didn't mean he didn't have it. Members of both families took shifts at the house for the first few days and nights to help.

Shawn describes this as simply being there for her loved ones. "I can't see how anybody could have done anything different. How would we have helped less? How could we have considered helping less?" she says.

John greatly appreciated the attention of family and friends and understood they simply wanted to help, but he and Joan were exhausted. Joan still needed to sleep up to 18 hours a day and John needed time to care for his own injuries. They quickly became overwhelmed by the constant stream of visitors.

Soon after bringing her home, John gathered the families to let them know that although he still needed their support and daily assistance, he was ready to take over the 24/7 care. The families would still be there for help and support when needed, but he and Joan would have some privacy for at least part of the day.

"Johnny said, 'OK, we're good on our own now,'" Shawn says. "They needed their time alone and to have someone there all the time—even if they are there to help—is like an intrusion."

Now that Joan was home and somewhat settled, John finally had time to grieve and begin the journey of coming to terms with the changes in his life. Until this point, he had largely forgotten to care for himself. He had spent every day at RIO with Joan, coming home exhausted to sleep on the couch because their bed was too big without her in it.

Still healing from his own injuries, he now had to cope with the idea that the woman he married was gone and a stranger had appeared in their home—a stranger who didn't always remember who he was and who needed him to fill the role of both caregiver and jailer. Even with her remarkable recovery, facing that he could never let his guard down seemed daunting.

Still, John found it hard to leave her side, checking on her multiple times a day while she slept. "I was afraid she was going to die in her sleep," he says, his voice trembling. "There were times when she scared me by jumping up to go do something and not thinking about being safe. She would just jump up and go. And with my gimpy leg, I would have to hobble after her and catch her to slow her down a bit."

At the same time, John took it in stride. "It wasn't that bad," John says modestly of his new role as caretaker. "Part of the reason it wasn't an issue was she needed to sleep so much."

As the days went on John, Joan and the families settled into an uneasy routine. Unsure of what the future held, all they could do was wait for Joan to begin her outpatient therapy and hope for the best. At times, the enormity of her injuries and length of time her recovery would ultimately take seemed almost too much to bear.

"It's like it is a big ball of ice, and it drips off a little at a time." Shawn says, explaining the frustratingly slow recovery process. As a result, the families were becoming hypervigilant, monitoring Joan's every move. Would she fall? Would she be overwhelmed by too much input as she moved through the world? Would she be overtired?

"No one could get near me when they came to the house without going through my sisters," Joan says.

"We all had to really guard her so that she got enough rest," Shawn explains. "She couldn't tell if she was too tired, so she would keep going if she didn't think she was done with what she was doing. Then her balance would get much worse, and her speaking would get harder to understand."

It was a delicate balance between guarding to ensure she didn't hurt herself and allowing her the autonomy to find her own way and to make her own mistakes. Joan desperately wanted her freedom, but the families couldn't let go. It was a vicious cycle.

John, who had no idea how he could help Joan's progress or what might damage her recovery, decided to take a hands-off approach. Rather than doing things for her, he let her do them on her own.

"The way I did it was letting her experiment, because I was experimenting too," he explains. "My attitude was, 'I'm not going to interfere unless she is going to hurt herself. If I see her trying to do something she is really struggling with, I'm going to ask her if she needs help. Other than that, I'm going to stay out of her way because I don't want to stunt her growth.' I was afraid I was going to do that if I interfered too much."

Not surprisingly, Joan agreed with the hands-off approach. "I can't pinpoint any direct thoughts about my feelings of people helping me, other than it wasn't necessary 'cause I didn't need help," she says. "The more someone would say I did need help, the more I knew that I could do it myself."

The rest of the people in Joan's life quickly jumped on this idea. "My family was really good about that. Short of hurting myself, they let me do what I wanted to do," Joan says.

They may have been willing to let her do her own thing, but finding that balance between helping and hindering didn't come easily. Still impulsive, Joan didn't always have the ability to make good decisions. She struggled with how to process steps, how to get from the beginning to the end of a task. Sometimes, she tried to skip the middle part entirely. The cost of letting her do things on her own meant those around her had to be constantly watching.

"One Friday night we had gone to Civic Stadium, and we were standing on the sidewalk waiting to cross the street. Joan got tired of waiting and walked out in front of a bus," John says. "I had to grab her by the collar and pull her back. It didn't just scare me; it scared the bus driver, too. It was a close call."

Still, John felt it was worth it. By allowing Joan the opportunity to do things herself, while still watching out for her, John and the families provided an environment that proved tremendously beneficial for Joan. "I always knew they had their eye open for me," Joan says. "If I was walking into the kitchen and not sure of my footing, there would be someone with their eye open."

Even while they were letting Joan explore and take risks on her own, acknowledging her limitations was crucial to her development. Those around her had to know where Joan was, both mentally and emotionally, at any given time, and adjust accordingly. Figuring out how to help without treating Joan like a child became a constant struggle.

Joan easily became overwhelmed by too much input, and she needed a constant calming presence. Having more than one or two people in the room could derail her, because it gave her too much to try to focus on. "I had to have calm," Joan says. "Slow speech, calm voice, but never being talked down to."

Luckily, Joan had Shawn to turn to for emotional support and acceptance. "By calmly accepting what I was doing and where I was at, Shawn validated what I was feeling. When I was chaotic, she was calm. The constant reassurance, the okays, the 'I love you,' it was complete and total serenity."

For Joan, the calmness Shawn offered helped her progress as much as any exercise a therapist could dream up.

"You're there almost as much for soul support as for physical support," Shawn said. "That to me is the biggest thing to give. Because you can hire a nurse to do all the other stuff, but it's the sharing of your soul that really makes the difference."

Joan adamantly agrees that Shawn's willingness to accept her made a huge difference. "She absolutely nailed it on the head. Because Shawn was able to reach in and really caress my soul and my heart and let me be who I was, coming out of wherever I came from, I was safe."

Joan had made it home. She had her family around her. She had her loving husband. She had her dog, when she remembered he existed. But she still had a long way to go.

Dr. Bruce

Being home didn't mean she had finished her rehabilitation work. On Aug. 3, 1999, Joan and her family had their first meeting with the staff at Community Re-Entry Service (CRS), where she would start her outpatient therapy. As she sat at the table with the doctors and therapists who would be taking over where RIO left off, Joan banged on the table and shouted "Let's get this going!" It was obvious to everyone in the room that this woman was going to be a handful.

Joan had slowly let go of her theories that she was a prisoner for the benefit of the unemployed, but she still wasn't entirely on board with the idea that she needed outpatient therapy. All she really understood was that a new group of people was saying she needed to fix something. Fine. She would fix it. As usual, her motivation came from proving there was nothing wrong. Joan, once again, had no idea how far she had to go.

Even with her remarkable recovery so far, Joan was a mess. She used a walker, slurred her words, couldn't track a conversation and was easily distracted. The staff at CRS planned to take over where RIO had left off, helping Joan continue to build her basic skills, like showering and dressing without help. Then they would continue with increasingly intensive physical and occupational therapy that would last for at least six months. In addition, they would provide counseling to help her come to terms emotionally with her situation.

Treatment at CRS would be much more intensive than that at RIO. While RIO focused on basic safety and health, CRS worked on problem solving and finding ways to reconnect the broken pathways between mind and body. This meant coming up with projects and exercises to teach her fine motor skills, such as grasping, pulling and manipulating small objects, puzzles, throwing a ball and paper maché projects. In other words, Joan had gone right back to Kindergarten.

Naturally, Joan protested. Gluing popsicle sticks onto a box was a demeaning task designed specifically to make her feel like a child, and she had already done that at RIO. She hated puzzles even before the crash, so the requirement to sit in a room and put them together was a torture dreamed up by sadistic therapists. As for those exercises in tossing a ball? What was she, a puppy? She refused to believe these exercises could help her and was exasperated that no one ever asked her if she enjoyed them.

"The fact that I had to do these things and had no say in the matter was belittling and humiliating," she says.

Joan also took issue with the program's focus on what she couldn't do rather than what she could. She didn't want to hear about what she had lost, because she didn't remember feeling differently before this. Instead, she wanted to know where she could go from here. Luckily, Joan had John at her side.

"Thank God for Husband," she says. "He made it OK for me to vent and voice my frustration. He was able to have it make sense to me as to why I had to do all this stuff. And you can bet he really didn't know all the reasons; however, he had the ability to trust the professionals."

John knew the physical therapists wanted to keep up with Joan's desire to be independent quickly and were going to up the ante to build her strength and balance. This meant torturous appointments that she came to dread.

"I had to wait in an outer office and know that what I had to do was not only going to hurt, but it would be frustrating," she says. "I recall walking to a table with a vinyl-covered pad, sitting down and the therapist holding my legs down while she instructed me to bend at my waist toward my toes. It was so hard. Everything hurt, and she had me repeat it a few times."

"Then it was time to work using the bars, kind of like you see gymnasts use, as my support and walk between them. I'll never forget thinking about the days I had to go to the gym and thinking I should be able to just do this without this entire struggle. I was always glad when my gym work was over. It was exhausting."

"The therapists were always positive and always praised me. However, because I wasn't what I thought I should be, the praises went in one ear and out the other."

"I wanted Husband. I could cry with him, and he wouldn't make me do anything I didn't want to or feel like doing. I could simply cry and ask him why this was so hard and why did they keep making me do things that hurt that I didn't want to do."

Although she didn't always understand the purpose behind what they were asking her to do, Joan did begin to bond with some of the staff, which went a long way toward easing the day-to-day frustrations. She even began to accept that some of them had her best interests at heart. Joan knew she had to get strength back in her arm and legs, so she was willing to cooperate with whatever her physical therapist, Katie, demanded, even when it was painful. Plus, she liked that Katie focused on improvement rather than loss.

"She encouraged me every step of the way. If I significantly struggled, she validated my struggle, backed it off and we moved on. I felt more of a desire to do things 'cause she believed in me, and I wanted to prove her right," Joan says.

It surprised Joan that the encouragement she received motivated her. "I wanted the feedback, the praise, whatever people were saying or doing to spur me on. I guess I wanted to prove to them I could do it and anxiously wanted their approval. Plus, I knew if they were on my side, I would get through the crap that much sooner and convince them I was good to go."

CRS also reinforced the idea that she could be responsible for her own success and taught her how to make that happen.

"All the therapy in the world wouldn't work if I hadn't accepted the fact that I had to do my own work at home," she says.

She took on the responsibility of pushing herself to keep improving and continue receiving that positive praise. She focused on finding things she could do without help, like finally conquering making the bed.

"I remember crying because I couldn't figure the steps out," she says. "I knew I had to keep going. I knew I could do it, and I saw the finish line."

Occupational Therapist Christine assigned to help Joan with writing and reading skills, became an encouraging confidant.

"She had a way of touching my heart and making sure I knew I was valuable and had a lot to share and could help others," Joan says fondly. Because of that relationship, Joan was willing to let Christine help her with her vision issues.

"My eyes were a real mess, with my right eye—the side that took the hits—now positioned far to the right and at an upward glance," she says. "My left eye was still in its original placement, where it was when I was born. However, I needed to hold anything I wanted to see up very, very close to my left eye to even attempt to see the words. No way could I read."

To make matters worse, although Joan could see light, color and shapes, her brain couldn't always make sense of what her eyes saw. Danyel White, a patient advocate at NW EyeCare Professionals, compares Joan's situation to a native English speaker traveling in a foreign country. She could hear the sounds of someone speaking. She just couldn't understand the words, because her brain no longer spoke the right language.

"Your eyes are in your body to be used as a team, and mine were on separate missions," Joan says. She saw two of everything, and when she moved her head, the images danced around in different directions. She had no depth perception, so she couldn't tell where things were. This meant she struggled with walking, because she had no idea how steep a hill was or how high the step.

As if double vision, ghosting images and not being able to understand what she was seeing weren't enough of a problem, Joan also suffered from light sensitivity. Danyel explains that although the cause for this sensitivity is not completely understood, it is one of the primary complaints of people with brain injuries, because of the huge effect it has on quality of life. Many survivors can't tolerate any light at all, and others, such as Joan, are affected only by bright lights.

These vision issues made setting a plan for her recovery even more challenging, because each problem needed a separate treatment. The therapists had to figure out if the issue was with her brain not processing information or her eyes not focusing on a visual cue.

To help, Christine worked on a plan to help her read the letters that seemed to jump and wiggle off the page, while other therapists worked on ways to help Joan determine how to compensate for her double vision. The process was frustrating for both Joan and her therapists, and Joan began to lose hope. Then Joan received even more bad news. Although the therapists could design plans to make it easier to function, there was not yet hope or treatment for correcting vision issues related to head injuries.

"I went in to see this *yahoo,* or should I say, *Dr. Yahoo.* He examined me, and his final analysis was,

'This is what you've got, and this is all you'll ever have.' I was stunned and heartbroken, not to mention scared shitless!" she says. "This neuro-ophthalmologist just kinda threw in the towel and said that was the way I was expected to go through life."

Fortunately for Joan, CRS Therapist Christine disagreed with this assessment. She suggested that Joan see Dr. Bruce Wojciechowski, an optometrist at NW EyeCare Professionals, who specializes in vision therapy and brain injuries.

"RIO gave me back my dignity; Dr. Bruce gave me back my world," Joan says of their Sept. 14, 1999, meeting.

Joan believes the vision therapy Dr. Bruce used played a major part in her extraordinary recovery. He began her treatment program by giving her a pair of glasses with a Fresnel prism attached to the right lens. This prism allowed her to see one image instead of two, retraining her brain to understand what her eyes were seeing. As a result Joan's double vision began to balance into one picture. He then added a series of eye exercises to create a form of physical therapy designed to teach her brain and her eyes to work together once again.

Thrilled by this simple-sounding treatment, Joan thought all she needed to do was put on a pair of glasses and move her eyes around a bit, and her vision would come back. Of course, it wasn't going to be that easy. Like every other form of physical therapy she had endured, these eye exercises were always exhausting, sometimes nauseating and often required several hours of naps after each session.

Frustrated that this was harder than she had planned, she also quickly became annoyed that she wasn't getting the results she wanted fast enough. Dr. Bruce tried to help her understand that vision therapy works inside the brain, on its own timeline, with no outward signs of recovery, and she simply must be patient. She wasn't buying it. As usual, she expected more than was realistic and felt guilty for not showing faster results.

"I had been in optics for years," Joan says, "which means I thought I knew more than I knew."

Slowly, but surely, Joan began to see results, which made her willing to work through the process, even if it took longer than she wanted.

"Eighty percent of your world is taken in through your eyes. If you can't see the hallway you are walking down, then walking isn't the biggest thing. But if you can see the hallway, you can see what you are headed toward," she says.

As she worked with Dr. Bruce, Joan realized his willingness to treat patients as people rather than conditions was just as important to her recovery as the funny-looking glasses. Dr. Bruce didn't see her as yet another patient with a brain injury. He saw Joan, the person. He allowed her to have an opinion and to be part of the decision-making process. He gave her a sense of being valuable, even if she wasn't perfect. He even listened to her suggestions about his vision-therapy process, even when she was completely off base.

"I tried to explain to him how to refract me," she laughs, referring to a commonly used procedure in optometry that she remembered from her work before the crash. "The cool thing about it is he said, 'Great idea!' instead of telling me I was wrong or stupid."

For Joan, this validation proved she could still offer an opinion, even if she was wrong. For the first time since the crash, in this one place, she felt like everyone else. Dr. Bruce not only helped her with her vision, he helped her see that she could be accepted, even as broken as she was. In him, she found someone who considered her to be a whole person with a bit of damage, instead of broken person who was someone less than before. The effect of his acceptance was unexpectedly profound. Joan began to think that maybe, just maybe, she could have hope for more acceptances in the future.

The Cuckoo Doctor

As she slowly improved, Joan found herself increasingly frustrated. She felt as if she had been split in two. There was Old Joan, who people said knew how to walk and talk and see straight. Old Joan had it all. She could balance her checkbook and knew not to run into the street in front of cars. Now, there was New Joan, who was not quite sure what to make of her confusing, erratic world. New Joan knew something was wrong, but couldn't quite put her finger on it. She desperately wanted to catch up and figure out what she was missing, but she didn't have a clue where to start. For this, she would need Dr. Gregory Cole, the man she calls her *Cuckoo Doctor*.

A clinical psychologist who specializes in the behavioral psychology of those with brain injuries, Dr. Cole's job was to help Joan understand that she had an injury she couldn't see and how that injury affected her emotions, memory and movement.

He began by working with Joan to help her accept the notion that she had lost some of her emotional abilities and memories because of damage to her brain. This is why, he explained, the people around her kept insisting she acted differently. That didn't mean there was something *wrong* with her. She had an injury that had hurt her brain and left gaps in her life, and he was there to help her understand the cause and effect of the injury.

To help Joan visualize what had happened, he explained that her brain before the crash was like a huge file cabinet filled with everything she had ever experienced. One drawer held folders full of her emotions, one of facts and the third of memories. Then one day, a tornado swooped down and sucked up the entire file cabinet.

When the wind died down, her cabinet had been ripped open and her folders scattered. Some landed nearby, and she could pick them up and put them back where they belonged. Others she had to look for, but would find eventually. Then there were those that simply blew away, gone forever. Moving forward meant accepting that her problems were because of the loss of all those files from the injury she had suffered. The only way Joan would be able to go forward was if she could make the connection between what files were left and what files needed to be refilled with new experiences and memories.

With this explanation came a needed emphasis on her current abilities and strengths rather than her losses. "When I met Dr. Cole, I knew for the first time in this whole ordeal that I was going to come out OK and that I wasn't stupid, dumb or not able to grasp what was going on around me," Joan says.

Getting Joan to accept the concept of a brain injury included helping her understand the magnitude of what she had been through and the impact it had on her day-to-day life.

"He validated my feelings," she says. "When you feel like you are going crazy, are losing your mind, it's not you, it's the injury. The injury is that big, that profound, that monumental, that it will try to run you.

You have to get a grip of who you are and run yourself."

When Joan became upset because she needed endless reminders to help her remember the world had changed, Dr. Cole helped her stop punishing herself. He helped her recognize that this frustration was counterproductive. He showed her how to connect forgetfulness with the brain injury instead of viewing it as a personal failing. He stressed the need to separate Joan the person from Joan's injured brain.

As Joan began to believe that there really was a physical explanation behind many of her issues, she also began to understand the difficulties she had controlling her emotions.

"I was still Joan, but there was a part of Joan that I couldn't control so well," she says. "To top it off, I thought that was the way everybody should handle things. My way was the *only* way. After all, they were more screwed up than I was, so I felt it necessary to 'help' them. It couldn't be all me, it just couldn't."

According to Dr. Cole, the damage to her brain, the missing files from her file cabinet, left Joan with the emotional development of an average toddler. She wasn't childlike, but she had lost the adult skills to process her emotions. The physical damage to the parts of the brain that controlled her emotions might not ever heal. If they didn't, her brain would need to find new pathways to avoid the damaged areas. She had to start all over again.

When Joan first awoke, she quickly figured out that if she demanded or fussed, she would get attention. In the hospital in Utah, she discovered the call button for the nurse and kept hitting it. When the nurse came in, Joan didn't need anything. She just did it because she could. It was an action that got a response, so she repeated it over and over, much to the nurse's despair.

Then she learned that if she yelled, people paid attention. It might not have been the most effective way to have her needs met, but it got results. Things changed when she reached RIO. There, if she yelled the staff would correct her, saying, "No Joan, don't yell. Do it this way next time."

If, when the next time rolled around, she could remember in the heat of the moment that there was another way, she would choose it. When she didn't remember, she screamed and shouted, only to be reminded again, "No Joan, do it this way."

This lack of control was exhausting for Joan and those around her. Every day brought something new, some new emotion or challenge or frustration that she lacked the skills to deal with.

"As she is healing, she is going to learn to manage her emotions more effectively, but a lot of it has to do with retraining and learning the skills," Dr. Cole says.

For Dr. Cole, much of this learning and retraining started with helping Joan make sense of this strange world she had been thrown into and understanding that she saw it with the eyes of a child. Dr. Cole looked beyond the broken and battered adult body and saw the frightened little girl inside. Of all the people in her life, he saw her not as a 40-something adult with a brain injury, but rather as the wounded child who had to learn to express herself appropriately when her feelings were hurt.

"I felt so comfortable because just like Dr. Bruce, Dr. Cole saw me as a person, not a condition," Joan says.

Because she could not remember how to calm herself down, for example, he taught her breathing exercises to use when stressed out or frustrated. He helped her learn to visualize a happy place where she could go to when she needed time to regroup. He taught her how to notice and respond to when she was feeling angry or upset.

Along with teaching Joan a variety of coping skills to move beyond her toddler years and into her teens, he also helped her to learn how to balance new experiences and emotions as she began the journey into adulthood.

I'm Not Disabled!

These techniques were a huge help, especially when it came to reconciling her version of reality with the one accepted by those around her. Since she had opened her eyes in Utah, Joan had insisted she was the same person she had always been, regardless of what those around her said. With Dr. Cole's help, she finally understood that she had suffered a brain injury and that was why she had such a conflict between understanding her present and her past. Joan's brain injury had severed her emotionally from her previous life, so it had no meaning for her.

When Joan thought about events in her past, she saw them as paintings she had seen on a wall. She recognized the picture and knew she had seen it before. It just didn't mean anything to her. It had no special significance for her life.

"I have long term memory, but I don't remember what it felt like, because this is the only life I've known. I have no emotional attachment. Although I can remember doing things from my past, like four years of cheerleading in high school, learning to swim as a little girl, fun stuff growing up and all the sibling rivalry junk, I have no feeling of it, no emotional recollection at all," she says.

This detachment played into her lost coping skills. Usually a person learns to cope with unhappiness and disappointment through a lifetime of emotional experiences. Joan, like many survivors of brain injuries, no longer had those emotional memories.

There were no hurt feelings that she conquered after being left out of a grade school birthday party or tearful resolutions after fighting with a high school boyfriend. For her, each distress or hurt feeling was the very first time it had happened and often left her clueless about how to cope. In her world, the natural reaction to a challenge was the same as any other kindergartner who lost her seat in musical chairs. "Dammit, give me back my seat!"

Along with teaching her the coping skills needed to process all these new feelings, Dr. Cole helped Joan understand she was someone valuable, rather than someone broken.

"He taught me to love the person I am," she says.

He routinely told her, "You're going to be fine. You may not be exactly the same person, but there are going to be parts of you that are the same person."

This doesn't mean it was easy. His office provided a safe place to fall, to learn how to go to a happy place and to learn general coping techniques, but it was also a place where she could be angry. And Joan had anger.

She couldn't stand it when people treated her as disabled. "They would talk to me l.i.k.e. t..h..i..s.." Joan says of many of the therapists she encountered. "They would say, condescendingly, 'You have a brain injury,' like they were talking to a 3-year-old, and I wanted to say, 'You will too, Buddy, if you keep talking to me like that!' and shake my fist at them."

Dr. Cole tried to explain there is a natural tendency to treat those with brain injuries as children, speaking down to them and making decisions for them rather than speaking slowly and helping them make their own decisions, but Joan wasn't buying it.

For her, this approach was inexcusable and resulted in the rebelliousness that in turn threatened her recovery. Joan couldn't stand the insistence of keeping her in a box as someone damaged. She didn't consider herself disabled, and anyone who suggested she should was asking for a fight.

"At times, one of the therapists would be talking to us in a very demeaning tone as if we were children," she says angrily. "I didn't want to work with him."

She felt like the people around her were defining her by this brain injury they insisted she had, rather than as the person she knew she was and they were completely focused on what she had lost. "Dammit. I don't even know what *it* is, but *it* is not defining me," she says. "I'm still this girl. I can still talk, although it may be coming out as mishmash. I would hear me being me."

Dr. Cole prefers a treatment program that focuses on what the patient can accomplish rather than on what has been lost. Without this approach, he believes the patient is left lacking belief in a future even if the rehabilitation care is otherwise excellent.

"It's important that we help them learn skills to respond to their deficit," he says, "but we also need to help them feel like they have some hope. The reason patients get pissed is that they are saying, 'I'm still a person. Would you please treat me like a person?'"

Dr. Cole helped John and Joan come to terms with Joan's reactions to the frustration of rehabilitation by constantly reminding them that her feelings were normal. He helped them understand that even an uninjured person with excellent coping skills thrown into an unfamiliar situation and asked to do belittling tasks may feel overwhelmed.

"Think of a person who has a brain injury and is trying to relearn some of these skills to manage these emotions, and multiply the level of frustration by 10," Dr. Cole says.

That frustration often leads to patients focusing on symptoms rather than the bigger picture. For example, instead of determining what they could do to relieve their depression, they focus on feeling depressed. Joan, on the other hand, was adamant about doing what she needed to do to move forward.

"Joan was different in comparison with many of the clients I've worked with because one, she was a fighter, and two, she really had a mind of her own that came through no matter what," Dr. Cole says. "Joan always had a really positive perspective about things."

He encouraged her to use humor to deal with her challenges because it is such a strong part of her personality. At one session, Dr. Cole asked what she liked to do in her spare time. "With a stone-cold face I said, 'Sit on the porch and shoot dogs. What do you do?'" Joan says.

Dr. Cole may have been amused by Joan's way of thinking, but not everyone at CRS considered her mindset beneficial. Her cheerfulness, coupled with her quirky sense of humor and her lack of inhibitions, landed her in hot water with more than one of her doctors and therapists. She was known for acting even more disabled than she was, walking into walls or freaking out in the office, just to see if she could get a rise out of various staff members.

Upsetting as it may have been for those who didn't understand her quirky sense humor; it was all part of helping Joan realize she could still have a life, even if she admitted she had a brain injury. To move on, Joan had to accept who she was now.

"With brain injury, and this is stressed a lot, the person you were is gone." Joan says.

This philosophy matched what Teresia had tried to teach her back at RIO, and it finally clicked. When Joan finally understood that she had a clean slate to write her life on, regaining the past was less important than living for the future. Teresia's mantra, *You don't get your old life back; you get a brand new life,* became Joan's.

"Dr. Cole made it OK for me to love the person I was now by helping me say goodbye to the Old Joan," she said. "That girl is gone, and now I need to know how to move forward."

No More Pity Party

Moving forward meant Dr. Cole needed to work with John and Joan as a couple, helping them to come to terms with the radical changes in their lives. After a brain injury, many marriages end in divorce, because the people involved cannot cope with their new reality. Sometimes, it's the spouse who chooses to leave, unable to accept the position of caregiver or cope with the emotional changes in their partners. Sometimes, it is the person with the brain injury who leaves, because her partner no longer fits into her world. Either way, the risk to a marriage is high.

John and Joan didn't believe they would split up because of their new reality, but it was reassuring to know that these challenges were a natural side effect of the situation.

Dr. Cole also worked with the couple on accepting that the changes were going to be coming for a long, long time. "During the first year of recovery after a TBI, you generally make the most progress," he told them. "That's generally when the most physiological change occurs with brain growth. But you're still going to experience further changes in the years to come."

Coping skills were going to be vital for both of them as they faced the inevitable conflicts as Joan *grew up*. "They {patients with brain injuries} are experiencing all the changes since the injury, so they are incredibly stressed by the fact that they are not the way they were before. Many also have family members who emphasize to them that they are not the way they were before," he explains. "Unfortunately, as many marriages fall apart, the individual with the brain injury becomes increasingly depressed. We certainly want them to move forward with their lives, so somehow we have to reinforce to them that there is hope."

Even though depression may be common for those with a brain injury, Joan didn't see herself going that route. "I don't know that I went through a depression, and I don't think I sat and wallowed. I forgave the drunk driver off the bat, then said, 'Dammit let's go!'"

This didn't mean she didn't struggle with the enormity of living her life. She had self-esteem issues, struggled with how she looked and worried about how others perceived her. The worst part was little she could do to change it.

"Because of my double vision, putting on makeup was a nightmare. Obviously, I couldn't put on mascara while wearing glasses." Since putting makeup on was difficult, she thought, "Why bother? So here I go into the world, bald or with peach fuzz, eyes pointing in two different directions and not able to even put on a little makeup to help me feel like I was even somewhat pretty. Maybe too much emphasis is put on physical beauty; however, when you don't even know who you are, you'd like to rely on something. Add to it that I was attempting to prove to myself and others that this was all okay, and I could handle whatever life threw me, even if it was a bone."

Joan and Dr. Cole worked out a plan. She would allow herself to have a "five-minute pity party" once a day. Each morning, when she first got up, she walked into her bathroom and set a timer for five minutes. She stood in front of the bathroom mirror and asked, "Why? Why was this happening to me? Why did I lose my old life? Why did I become this person? Why did I have to suffer?"

"I still mourned that I was unable to do things that I knew were once simple for me," she says. "At times, I felt trapped in a body by a brain that could no longer function well and would shut down whenever and wherever it wanted. I didn't know what was expected of me and how I would handle it if I let someone down or screwed up big time. I knew those times were going to be a part of my life. For a person who could always depend on herself to get things done that needed to be done, this sucked!"

"What happened if I forgot an appointment or someone's name?" she wondered. "What do I say to them? What will they think of me? What if something, God forbid, happens to Husband, and I have to stack hangers for a job? Why the hell did this happen to me? I can't balance a checkbook or use the call waiting function on the phone. Basic math is no longer basic. If I don't have a calculator, I can't add or subtract, and let's totally forget trying to divide. Everything that I used to do easily, I can't now, and it sucks!"

As the time ticked away, Joan looked herself in the eye and talked about everything making her miserable. She allowed herself to talk, to rant, rave and cry about everything that bothered or scared her. She would ask why her husband and family had to suffer along with her. She would even include the struggles of the dedicated staff trying to help. Then the timer would go off, and her day would begin. For the next 24 hours, whenever a thought crossed her mind that fell into the category of pity, it had to wait until the next morning for her five-minute pity party.

This went on for several weeks. "One day, I was walking by the mirror in the living room, looked in it and stopped. I pointed and smiled at myself and said, "Because you're worth it!" That was the last day of my pity parties and a new beginning for me, mirrors and self-worth. I had a new game to play. Every time I'd walk by a mirror—it didn't matter where I was at—I'd point and say, 'Because you're worth it!'"

To celebrate her new mindset, Joan decided to cut the wisp of hair on the back of her head. That small curl, left behind when Dr. Welling shaved her head in Utah, was the last connection to the person she had once been.

"I kept that wisp there for quite a long time, feeling as if it was a testimony of what I had been through," Joan says. "What I didn't realize at the time was that little wisp of hair was actually holding me back. It probably wasn't just the wisp; however, I was justifying things that were hard or new to me, and all I had to do was look at that wisp, and it made everything I was feeling or had to go through concrete."

It was time to sever that connection to Old Joan's life. Grabbing her scissors, she cut the wisp of hair and screeched to John that they were going shopping. She wanted to buy pretty hats to keep her bald head warm and give her a bit of style.

"No more hiding bald-headed Joan," she shouted. "This new girl still had spunk, and I was out to show that to the world!"

Cutting her hair was a defining moment. This was the day Joan decided to embrace who she was.

"I felt so damned proud of myself for doing that. I figured if the New Joan is going to get anywhere, then no part of the Old Joan could hold her back. It truly was a feeling of release. I had a new-found energy and there was nothing that was going to stop me now. I knew if there was something I wanted to do—that was, of course, safe—then I might need to find a new and different way to go about it. However, the end result could be just as exciting as the beginning."

It was time for Joan to discover what that end result would be.

I Feel Good

In February 2000, Joan bounced into her final CRS assessment carrying a CD player blasting the song *I Feel Good* by James Brown. The staff cheered and laughed as Joan spun and twirled around the conference room, shaking hands and giving out hugs as she thanked them for everything they had done. The joy on the faces of the doctors, therapists and counselors was obvious as they watched their miracle girl dance around the room. She might still be unsteady on her feet and difficult to understand, but she had progressed beyond their wildest dreams.

Joan had come to CRS to say goodbye to those who had worked so hard to help her succeed. Her recovery had reached a point where she was ready to take the reins and regain control of her life. Shawn beamed as she watched Joan ping from person to person hugging and saying her goodbyes. John, waiting patiently in the background as usual, smiled and softly chuckled. She might have been different in many ways from the woman he married in 1992, but she was still his rambunctious Joan. They were both ready to leave CRS and all the doctors behind and begin the next phase of their lives together.

Excited about her release from the drudgery of her rehabilitation sessions at CRS, Joan quickly ran into trouble. As much as she hated going, her outpatient therapy gave structure to her life. Without the CRS staff guiding her with suggestions and demands three times a week, her day became a mundane routine of exercise, TV watching, napping and waiting for John to come home. Sitting around had never suited the active Joan, and it didn't take her long to figure out that it was up to her to be proactive if she wanted out of the house.

"One can only watch so much TV," Joan says. "I was made to talk, and as my mother always said, 'The body is made to move, so get out there and move.'"

Even scarier, Joan knew that if she stayed on this path of inactivity, she would end up as nothing more than a statistic. "I felt that if I just stayed at home without meeting or interacting with new people, I may possibly slump into some kind of thinking that I couldn't do anything, thus taking on society's role of what I couldn't do because of the TBI. I wasn't about to let that happen! I knew I had to keep stimulating my brain. I needed to engage with people."

She wanted to find something to do, but what was out there for her? Although Joan refused to consider herself as someone disabled, the truth was that she barely functioned as an adult. Getting a job, even a part time one, wasn't an option because of her challenges with processing information and her limited ability to speak and reason. Then there was the fatigue that overwhelmed her after only a few short hours of activity, reducing her chances of gainful employment even more. It looked like returning to the real world was going to be harder than she realized.

One day as she sat on the couch mulling over her lack of a future, she suddenly remembered the advice Teresia Hazen had given her during her treatment in the Healing Garden. Rather than try to find a job, she could become a volunteer.

"Volunteering is a great work role," Teresia had told her. "It is a service to the community, and it helps people take care of that need to do work."

A volunteer position could help Joan find a sense of purpose without the pressure of a real job. She could build a schedule that accommodated her fragile body and need for daily naps while still giving her the sense of accomplishment she longed for. Plus, it would get her back out into the public and interacting with people. Because brain injury or no brain injury, Joan was determined to regain her place as a social butterfly, and that meant getting out into the world.

John laughingly agreed, saying, "One of the main reasons Joan decided to get active is just her personality. She is very social, and she needs that. Keeping her in the house alone was not an option. I knew she had to do it, because of who she is. If she didn't do it, she would wither."

Joan had just started looking for opportunities when a friend casually mentioned that The Cellar Gift Shop at Good Samaritan was looking for volunteers. It was almost as if it was meant to be. Not only were the staff at The Cellar experienced at working with those with brain injuries, the proceeds from sales went directly to assisting patients going through rehabilitation at RIO. Joan was beside herself,

"This way, I was truly giving back to RIO for all they did for me" she says.

She contacted The Cellar the next day to make arrangements for a volunteer orientation and soon had a start date in her calendar.

As she considered this huge step she was about to take, Joan was torn between excitement and fear. For the first time since the crash, she would be venturing out on her own, without the safety net of her family to help if things went wrong. She would have to rely on herself, make her own decisions and choose her own path. She would have to use all of the skills she had learned over the past few months to stay on track and keep herself safe. She would have to be ready to ask for help when she needed it, accepting that she would be in many situations she would be unprepared for. Luckily, New Joan felt no disgrace in being afraid or not knowing the answers.

"Husband really, really, pounded that into my head, figuratively," Joan says, giving John credit for helping her accept her limitations. She believed that as long as he supported her idea of volunteering, she would be fine.

John might have been supportive, but seeing Joan start down this new path was also terrifying. He wanted to encourage her independence, but he worried whenever Joan was out of his sight. The thought of her being out on her own, surrounded by people who might not understand her needs, made him reluctant to support her desire for freedom. He or another member of the family had been at her side every time she had left the house since she had come home.

Now, for the first time, Joan would be alone, and he wasn't sure he was ready for that. He worried about all of the things that could go wrong. What if she got scared and started to panic? Who would help her? What if she got lost? What if she got sick? Who would she turn to if he wasn't there?

He tried to make light of his fears, reassuring himself that she would be in a familiar place. "I knew she was in a safe place, and she wouldn't have any problem asking for help if she needed it. It wasn't like she was going out playing on the freeway," he says.

In his heart, John knew that he was lucky that Joan had chosen Good Samaritan as the place to begin her journey into the world. The hospital staff was trained to deal with people with disabilities, and if she ran into problems, Joan could simply go up the elevator to RIO, quickly returning to a familiar, safe environment. He couldn't have asked for a better place for her to begin to stretch her wings and fly.

He had to take a deep breath and let her go. He had to put aside his fears and support Joan. He might be worried, scared and unsure, but there was no way he was going to let her see it. For the first time since the crash, Joan was excited and hopeful about something new, and John was not about to try to stop her. No matter how much it scared him.

After deciding where she wanted to volunteer, Joan's next challenge was going to be how to get there. Joan had been relying on John, Shawn and other family members to get her wherever she needed to go. It was time for her to show her independence by making her own transportation arrangements. She contacted the LIFT, a bus service provided for people with disabilities through the Tri-Met Bus service in Portland, and arranged her first ride.

"I think I was more nervous about riding the LIFT than I was anything else," she says, "because I didn't know what to expect. The whole idea of getting on a bus was foreign to me." She had so many questions. How did she get on the bus? Would it come to the house? How did she pay? Would the driver understand her needs? Plus, the idea of putting her trust in someone other than a family member or friend to get her safely to her destination was disconcerting.

"The fact that I was able to have freedom was great, but I was scared to death. I did feel more independent knowing I had a way to get out in the world. I now had the means of mobility and would be forced to learn something and be uncomfortable for a while," she says. But she was sure it would be worth it if she wanted to continue to grow.

The idea of Joan riding the LIFT gave John a whole new series of things to worry about. He obsessed about her being in a vehicle driven by someone he didn't know. It didn't matter to him that this was a professional driver and not some guy from down the street. He was still being asked to entrust his wife's safety to a stranger. What if they crashed? What if they dropped her at the wrong place? Would they take care of her? Once again he had to force himself to hide his fear, pretend he was okay with her choices, and breathe.

"I knew she wasn't going to be doing anything solo, that she would be with someone trained. I was worried, but I wasn't panicked."

As John worried silently, Joan fought her own battle against misconceptions. She shocked John by admitting that one of her biggest concerns was what the neighbors might think when the LIFT pulled up to their front door. Although most of the neighborhood knew Joan had been in a horrible accident, few had information on how severe her injuries were. She was embarrassed they would think she was so incapable that she needed the special bus. Joan believed she looked perfectly normal, and she worried the neighbors would think she didn't deserve special treatment. She was oblivious to how she appeared to the rest of the world, not realizing her balance and depth perception issues and inability to walk down the stairs was obvious to anyone who saw her.

Joan's greater worry was what the neighbors would think about John when they saw her board the bus. The last thing she wanted was for anyone to think poorly of her loving husband who had been through so much.

"I thought they might think that John wasn't taking care of me and that he wouldn't take me to where I needed to be. That he was going off to work and I had to have this special transportation because he can't take me. I was afraid they would think he was a schlep!"

John laughed when Joan told him about her fear of the neighbors thinking badly about him for choosing his job over her. He had fought his own demons of doubt when he first returned to work a few weeks earlier. Leaving her alone so he could go back to work had almost crushed him.

"The first time I went back to work was really hard, and I was only working half days. I drove down the street in tears," he admits. Now, Joan was going to be out on her own without him. It was both unnerving and thrilling.

When the long awaited day of volunteering finally arrived, a scared and excited Joan was up at the crack of dawn waiting for her ride. She couldn't wait to go.

"I gave myself permission to feel nervous," she says. "What I had to do with the LIFT is to convince myself that this was my step back into the world. It was my way back into the world. I had to walk through this uncomfortableness to be comfortable."

When she saw the small Lift bus pull into her driveway, Joan worried how she would get to it. Even though she had been practicing every day, and Dr. Bruce's vision therapy and prism glasses were helping, it would be a long time before she could safely navigate the stairs out of her house, or her driveway, without help. To her relief, when the driver came to the door, he knew exactly what to do to help her.

He understood that walking out the door and locking it behind her was a slow, step-by-step process. The driver patiently waited while she slowly opened the screen door, walked onto the stoop, turned around, closed the door, locked the door, put her keys in her purse and turned back around to face him, taking time to think out each step before she moved to the next. He then took her by the arm and guided her down the two steps to the sidewalk and down her slightly sloped driveway to the waiting bus.

After the driver helped her up the steps into the bus and secured her for the trip to Good Samaritan, Joan took a deep breath and congratulated herself for overcoming her fear. She had done it! She was on the bus and settled in for her adventure. Then it struck her. For the first time since Utah, she was in a vehicle being driven by someone who wasn't part of her family.

"I didn't know this driver, and here I had just survived this horrific car crash, and I was supposed to put my life in this person's hands."

Joan was terrified, but reassured herself that it was a quick trip to the hospital. After all, when she went with John or Shawn, it only took 20 minutes to get there. She concentrated on her breathing, used all Dr. Cole's calming techniques and reminded herself she could do this. But she had no idea how long this bus ride would be.

The reservations clerk at the LIFT had warned her that they had a two-hour window for travel time, but Joan didn't understand what that meant. She had no idea she was only the first stop on a long route that sent the bus around town picking up other passengers. Instead of a quick run down the freeway, she spent over an hour in her seat, constantly looking out the window worrying they would be hit by a car.

She finally made it to the hospital, and the driver helped her out of the bus and into the front doors. Joan took a deep breath, turned to the left and walked down a short hall to The Cellar for her first day. She had arrived.

The Cellar

To ease her into the volunteering process, the coordinator assigned Joan a two-hour shift filled with simple tasks. "At the beginning it was just kind of getting to know the store. Look around, see what we have, talk to people, that type of thing," Joan says.

Although she was working with a staff experienced in helping people with disabilities rejoin the working world and someone was always nearby to guide her, each thing she did seemed monumental. Even a trip to the nearby restroom became a complicated adventure. There may have been signs showing her how to get to the restroom from The Cellar, but there was nothing showing her how to get back.

"I couldn't go there on my own," she says, "because I would have gotten lost on the way back. It might say restroom on the sign with an arrow pointing the right way, but how far down the hall does that arrow go? And by the time I got down to the end of the hall, the chances were I forgot where I was going."

Joan laughs as she recounts the challenges she had with something as simple as bathroom stall doors. She could only use the handicap stalls, because she knew those doors opened out. If the door opened in, chances were she would hit herself in the head with the door when she tried to leave.

"Going to the bathroom ain't fun," she says ruefully. "I'd ram the door into my shoulder and then fall back into the toilet."

Halfway through her first shift, she walked to the cafeteria with one of the staff to get a snack. What happened next was terrifying.

"My heart is racing just talking about this," she says as she remembered the frightening experience.

She walked into a normal, brightly lit cafeteria, filled with stacks of food and containers, shiny counters, groups of tables and chairs, chatting, laughing people and banging silverware and dishes. It was the same kind of lunchroom found in every school, hospital and big business across America. She had been going to them since she was a child, so it should have been easy.

It wasn't.

"It was mortifying," she says. "Visually, there was just so much."

For Joan it was complete overload. The lights were so bright she couldn't focus, and the noise was overwhelming. There was so much to look at that her eyes, trying to send too much information to her brain, left her unable to process what she saw. She couldn't tell where things were. She could see tables and chairs, but because of her depth perception issues, she couldn't tell exactly where they were. Was that chair close enough to trip over, or was it on the other side of the room?

Then she got to the counter and had to place an order. Again, this should have been simple. She had been ordering food in a cafeteria line since she was in grade school. How hard could it be? To her shock, it was almost impossible.

"I had to make a decision about what I wanted on my sandwich. All of a sudden, I had all these choices, and it was too much," she says. "Wheat or white bread? Ham or turkey? American or Swiss? Do I write down what I want? Can I choose anything? It's all the same price? That's way too much information! Everything was just huge. There was just too much."

Joan was ready to run screaming for the nearest exit, but she had no idea how to get there. She finally made it through lunch and returned to the gift store to complete her short day. Then it was time to take the LIFT home.

"That was frightening, too," she says. "They told me I had a 'pick-up time window,' and I didn't know what that meant. I freaked out that I was going to miss the bus, and if I miss this bus, I would have to call John."

She wasn't sure if the driver would come and get her or if she needed to wait outside. Would they be able to find her? What if they couldn't? Would they leave without her? How would she reach John for help if they forgot her?

"There's no way I could get home!" she worried.

The LIFT reservations clerk had explained the driver would come in and get her, but with all she had been through during that first day, Joan forgot her instructions.

"Explaining something to you and physically experiencing it are two different things," Joan says.

Just as she started to panic, she turned around and found the driver patiently waiting for her at The

Cellar door. He walked her to the bus, and they started the long drive home.

By the time she got back to her house, she was exhausted, even though she had only been gone for about four hours. She called John to tell him she was home safely and went to bed, where she stayed until he came home.

"She was pretty much toast for the rest of the night and into the next day," John says, commenting on the aftermath of Joan's first short, successful, venture into the world.

When she got up the next morning, she realized she couldn't wait to do it again. Proud of herself for conquering her fear, she knew she had begun her journey back to independence.

As the weeks went on, Joan got into the swing of things, moving from greeting people to stocking shelves, dusting and learning to work the cash register. Her skills slowly improved, which led to the assignment of increasingly difficult duties and tasks. The more she worked, the more her confidence and ability to accept making mistakes grew.

Many of her challenges and errors come from her limited ability to communicate. She often has to stop and think about what she wants to say, and it is hard to stay on track. Simple things can derail her, such as having a conversation peppered with pronouns. When *Mike* turns into *he* or *Jan* becomes *she*, Joan easily loses track of who is being referenced.

"When people use pronouns throughout a conversation or when more than one name has been mentioned, I have no idea who they were talking about," she says. Often, by the time Joan figures out it is the same person, she will have lost track of the entire conversation.

"It was really hard at first to ask people to explain things," she says. "I needed things broken down into really simple terms and phrases. Many times, I used to just nod and try to keep a blank look off my face in fear they might lose their patience or think I'm stupid."

People often become frustrated by her struggle to get words together in a coherent sentence and her fragmented train of thought. One cranky person she worked with even told her she shouldn't be talking to people because she was confusing to listen to. But Joan wasn't about to let the naysayers get her down. "I'd talk to anybody at any time. No one was going to shut me up. No one," she says.

Unlike her days in RIO, when she had to prove everyone else wrong, Joan had learned to let things go. "I'd grown a lot since then," Joan says. "When deciding that I wanted to get back amongst people again and join the world, I knew I was going to be making mistakes."

Shawn was amazed at the changes in Joan when it came to accepting her need for help. She remembered the days before the crash when Joan would get defensive about not knowing the answer to an obscure question. Now, she didn't even seem to notice when she had to ask for help to find the bathroom.

"After the brain injury, she didn't remember feeling stupid, so she could express the intelligent Joan that she was all along. The injury took away the negative talk," Shawn says.

Being back in public and dealing with people also gave Joan a chance to practice the conflict and anger management skills Dr. Cole had worked so hard to teach her. "Knowing there was going to be conflict and that I could make the choice of either being combative, which was getting me nowhere, or walking away was like, 'WOW! A success!' So I was building on success."

Joan quickly realized her attitude and willingness to try to communicate was being noticed. She wasn't a disabled clerk working in a gift store. She was a survivor demanding that the rest of the world see her on her terms. For those visiting family and friends in the hospital, she was becoming an inspiration.

"While at The Cellar I was able to experience firsthand how I was able to make a difference by meeting and talking with customers who were under some sort of stress or anguish about a loved one and needed a pair of nonjudgmental ears to listen and hugs to prove to them I cared."

When it came to those with someone in RIO, Joan was a beacon of hope. In her they could see that recovery could happen. Instead of a disabled casualty, they saw someone who beat the odds and came out on the other side. They asked questions about her injury and her treatment, and she gave answers. Long past her conspiracy theories, Joan wanted to share with the world that RIO was the place that saved her. Her first mission, to raise awareness of the treatments of brain injuries, was building steam.

"I had an opportunity to be the success story from RIO to anybody else coming in. I came from RIO. The therapy at RIO was rigorous. It's tough love. I came in crumpled. I was wheeled in and walked out. This was the kind of care they gave us," she says. Plus, interacting with these people, meaning something to them, was helping Joan in her continuing recovery. The social butterfly had found a new outlet.

As her confidence continued to grow, she began to push herself by exploring outside the safety of the store. She had always loved wandering, and now she challenged herself to get around without help.

"I got lost all the time," she says. She knew her adventurous streak was paying off the first time she found a destination without help. "I was able to find my way to the cafeteria and back, which was huge," she says proudly.

Joan had been at The Cellar for about six months when she began to get restless. Far from seeming as complicated as they had in the first few weeks, her job duties seemed low key and quiet. As her comfort level increased, she found she wanted more interaction and bigger challenges. She just wasn't sure where to look.

Joan Starts to Wander

As before, the opportunity presented itself the moment she was ready. One afternoon, the head of the volunteer organization approached Joan and asked her if she wanted to join in a new venture. They were going to open a flower cart in the lobby at Good Samaritan and needed volunteers to staff it. Of course, Joan jumped at the chance and quickly called John to let him know she had been personally chosen for this new experience. "Joan was very excited," John says with a smile.

"The thought of being in the main lobby of the hospital and having the opportunity to interact with so many people sold me right off the bat," Joan says. "I was very excited about this. This was very, very cool. I'm doing something that is going to bring someone happiness."

Located at the front entrance of the hospital, the flower cart provided Joan an entirely new range of duties, experiences and challenges that were going to be both physically and mentally harder than anything she had attempted before. The coordinator assigned her a mentor, Susan, who showed her how to set up the cart and arrange the flower bouquets.

"I loved working with Susan and learning names of flowers, being around the smells, watching people's reactions when Susan created bouquets in front of them, making people smile when delivering the flowers. It was a wonderful place to be," Joan gushes.

Joan started each day by going to the storage room to get the cart, bring it to the lobby and open up all the nooks and crannies for showing off the flowers. Then she went back to the storage unit to gather the day's flowers, which added a new mental challenge.

"I had to break up the flowers and put them in different buckets by size and shape, then bring them to the cart. I broke a lot of vases because of my depth perception issues. I couldn't judge where I was trying to set it down, so I would miss the spot and drop it on the floor. Then there was using the walkie-talkie, which wasn't hard to use as long as I remembered where I put it down," she says.

Eager to learn, she quizzed Susan constantly about every aspect of her job. When a customer had a question she couldn't answer, she was completely comfortable asking for help. "I wanted to make sure all questions got the correct answer," Joan says. "It was more challenging all the way around. It was a test that I gave to myself to see if I could do it."

One unexpected benefit of being part of a brand new venture was that everyone was struggling right along with Joan. "I gave myself permission to mess up because everyone else was messing up."

As her skills and comfort level increased, she asked to take over the task of delivering flowers to patients' rooms. Learning to navigate the multiple buildings in this major metropolitan hospital became her next adventure. The individually numbered buildings, attached by sky bridges, had rooms labeled on a directional system, meaning patients were not just in room 412, but in 4-SW 412. This could be confusing to those without a brain injury. For someone who struggled to remember how to get to the cafeteria on a route she traveled every day, this was going to be the challenge to end all challenges. Joan couldn't wait.

John, however, was not as thrilled. Although he understood that wandering the endless halls of the hospital would allow Joan to practice her freedom in a safe environment, he still worried.

"She's just very unselfish and tends to trust too much," he says. He feared that Joan's tendency to take people at their word put her at risk of those who might not have her best interests at heart. At the same time, John knew that as long as she stayed inside the boundaries of Good Samaritan, there would always someone watching out for her. Plus, she had agreed to John's request that she would never go outside the building unless it was with him, a member of the family or the LIFT driver.

To help John feel more secure, Joan came up with a way to ensure she could stay inside the parameters he set. If she found herself in a position that didn't make sense or might be uncomfortable, she would ask herself, "What would Husband think about what I'm going to do?"

If she came to the conclusion that her decision would make John uncomfortable or uneasy, she would choose a different path. By using John's thought process as her base Joan knew she could stay safe even if she didn't quite understand the situation. "For example, if someone asked me to come to the parking garage, or even to just come with them, I knew to say no because that is what Husband would want me to say."

This line of reasoning allowed John to once again take a deep breath and Joan was off and running. Over the next few months, Joan happily spent hours wandering the hospital, struggling to find her way from banks of elevators, through endless hallways and past hundreds of room numbers to find her destination.

"When I had to deliver flowers to someone in a different building other than the main hospital, it sometimes got a bit challenging and was always confusing. I went there via the sky bridge and had some landmarks, such as the Cellar where I had once volunteered, but I still managed to get turned around."

"Often, I would need to ask where a certain area was, using the floor reference, not the directional thing. Sometimes, I couldn't find my way back to the elevators, so I'd pop into an office, asking if someone there could point me in the right direction. If the directions were a two-or three-step process, I could almost count on having to stop and ask again after I completed each step because I wasn't able to retain the entire procedure. *Good thing I'm not a surgeon, huh?*"

Even when completely lost, frustrated and confused, it was all worth it when she finally reached her destination and saw the delight on the face of the surprised patient.

"Whenever I delivered flowers, I tried to remember to greet the person by using the name on the card and introduce myself to make the whole transaction a bit more personal. That wasn't something I was told to do;

it was my way of making it more comfortable for the patient. I wanted them to know that I, and Good Sam, cared and wanted to make their stay as comfortable as possible."

If getting there was half the fun, getting back was yet another adventure. Once she arrived at the correct room, she had to figure out which way to turn when she came back out. "Every time I walked out a door, I turned right, no matter what," she says.

She knew that to get back to the lobby, she had to find the right elevator to take her to the first floor. If she chose the wrong one, she would end up on the opposite end of the hospital and have to find her way back to the lobby. While Old Joan would have been frozen in fear, afraid of looking stupid, this new, adventurous Joan took it in stride.

"It frustrated me, but didn't panic me or make me feel stupid," she says. "Being lost had become normal."

It also put Joan in an unexpected place to help others.

"Getting on an elevator at the wrong bank of elevators was disconcerting, but it paid off one time. I took the wrong set of elevators and was heading back to the volunteer office when I heard a child wailing. It was obvious this child needed help and was standing right by the bank of elevators I had just stepped off of. I immediately turned around and went back to the child, told her my name and asked what was wrong."

"She told me the doors closed before she could get on with her mom's friend and she was terrified. I told her my name and that I volunteered at the hospital and that's why I was wearing this blue smock and that I'd sit with her and wait until her mom's friend came back to get her. She calmed down and was now just whimpering. A man stepped off the elevator and asked the little girl if she was Jane, to which the girl answered, 'Yes.

"He then said, 'Your mom's friend is looking for you and is on the floor where your mom is. I can take you to her.'

"I asked the little girl if she knew this man, and when she replied, 'No.' I thanked him and said, 'She'll be staying with me until her mother's friend comes to get her.' He thanked me as well and said he'd go up and let her know. He got in the elevator, and immediately the other one opened and the little girl's mother's friend frantically ran out calling out to her. I then asked the little girl if this was her mommy's friend. She said, 'yes,' so I was comfortable letting her go.

"The little girl started crying again, because she was so relieved, I imagine. In fact, they were both crying. I said to the little girl, 'I think this calls for some ice cream, and the cafeteria has great ice cream.' She was thrilled, and the woman couldn't stop hugging me and was now really crying hard and repeatedly thanking me."

"Later that week, Ginger, the volunteer coordinator, wanted me to read a letter she received. It was from the mom, thanking me profusely for the tenderness and concern I showed for her daughter. It brought tears to my eyes. That was a great outcome from taking the wrong bank of elevators!"

Another unexpected benefit of her endless journeys through the hospital was that it gave Joan ample time to visit with the staff and patients. "Delivering flowers not only gave me the opportunity to make someone smile, it allowed me to chat with people who were sometimes quite lonely and let them just talk," she says. She began to realize that taking the time to stop to say hello, share her story and listen to theirs made people happy. People responded to her childlike innocence and joy, sometimes with surprising results.

"One day around Christmas when I was at the flower cart, a woman walked by and had on the greatest Christmas sweater I had ever seen," she says. "It had penguins on it. I love penguins, and the colors were so bright and happy. While she was looking around I commented on how it was such a great sweater, in fact the greatest Christmas sweater I'd ever seen, and it made me smile just looking at it. She thanked me, did her shopping then went about her business in the hospital.

"When she was leaving, I commented once again, saying, 'There goes the happy sweater. I'm in a happy place now, and it's all because of your sweater.'

"I had stuff to do elsewhere in the hospital, so I left the cart and did my running around. When I returned, there was a wrapped package on the counter. I immediately told Susan she shouldn't have gotten me anything for Christmas. She said, 'Ahhhh just go ahead and open it.' When I opened the package, lo and behold it was the sweater the lady was wearing. I couldn't believe it! I immediately asked Susan where the lady was, and Susan replied, "She left with explicit instructions you were not to try and find her. She wanted to give it to you because it gave you so much joy."

The joy that Joan found in talking with the people around her made her wonder if she could do even more with her life.

Joan and the Kids

The idea of doing more sounded simple, but would it be? Joan may have been up for the challenge of doing something different, but she feared she would once again struggle to find somewhere to fit in. Who would want her? After all, she still wobbled when she walked, had trouble communicating and tired quickly. She still looked funny, with eyes that pointed different directions. Add in the concerns about transportation and navigating the outside world, and she and John both wondered if there would be any new opportunities for her to experience.

As luck would have it, they didn't have to wonder for long. A few quick inquiries showed that volunteer opportunities abounded in the Legacy Health System. Instead of starting the volunteer process over, she could simply add a new position. After looking into available options, Joan decided her next stop would be the Pediatrics Ward at Good Samaritan's sister hospital, Legacy Emanuel.

Joan had a soft spot for the kids in the hospital system. She often saw parents pulling them around in the hospital's little red wagons. She always made a point of stopping to talk with them, asking questions that showed an interest in something other than their illness.

She felt connected to these children. Like them, she had a hard time grasping what was happening around her and often struggled to catch up to what the "adults" were saying. She knew how devastating it was to not understand what was happening.

She admired the children's ability to overcome their struggles and to keep their boundless enthusiasm in the face of enormous challenges. They were fighting for their futures, and she felt a kinship with them. Volunteering in their world made sense.

Understanding her injury, the volunteer coordinator started her once a week with simple tasks. Her first assignment involved making three pots of coffee in the morning and stocking the snack cart. Then she would wander the hospital halls offering free goodies to parents who spent their days waiting for test results. It sounded so simple that Joan assumed she would have it down in no time flat. After all, she had a tremendous amount of practice stocking shelves and wandering Good Samaritan to deliver flowers. How difficult could it be?

It was harder than she expected. She forgot that the reason she had started looking for something new was because her duties at the flower cart had become boring and she had become too comfortable in her routine. She forgot that branching out meant creating memories for new places, new responsibilities and new duties. Something as simple as remembering where the supplies were kept became an exercise in frustration. Which cabinet did she go to for the coffee? Where were the candy bars kept? She had gone back to square one, and she wasn't happy.

Her new responsibilities required a mind shift. Still irritated by the difficulties she faced, she had to remember to give herself credit for how quickly she learned. Instead of focusing on failures, such as forgetting where the candy bars were, she celebrated the success of working the coffee pot.

"I stopped expecting so much out of myself and convinced myself that I was here to help and didn't need to produce anything of any significance. Everything was free, and the simple gesture of giving someone something to munch on or a cup of hot coffee was good enough. When I took the pressure off myself, I was much more relaxed and could really enjoy what I was doing."

Joan also quickly realized that her role in this particular place was more than passing out snacks and coffee. Up to this point, her audience had consisted of adults who wanted to talk about illness and injuries. Now, her audience comprised of children who wanted a friend. For Joan, this was a breath of fresh air. These kids didn't care that she looked funny or didn't walk in a straight line. They didn't see someone who wasn't good enough for the rest of the world and who was just trying to find a place to fit in. These children simply saw a new playmate.

"I was a friendly new face that wasn't going to poke, prod or stick 'em, so they wanted me to stay," Joan explains. "I guess they felt I was normal, and I could talk kid stuff, so they were happy and wanted me there."

The children accepted her as she was, wonky walk and all. In return, they demonstrated how living well *despite* a challenge was just as important as living well *with* a challenge.

"I met some really brave kids at Emanuel. One of the most positive things I got out of being on the children's ward was their strength. They wanted to be out playing. They didn't want to be in the hospital. They were gonna get better. They were so much more above the adults."

Surprisingly, the parents of those brave kids needed her as well. In Joan, they found someone who saw their children as kids who wanted to play, rather than children who might be dying. And Joan was always up to a good game of catch or Candyland.

"There are playrooms set up on the floor, and often I would go in offering parents a snack or coffee and would be asked by a child if I wanted to play with them," Joan says. "I never turned that offer down, so I got to play all kinds of games, whether they were in the room or made up. It gave me a chance to use my imagination—that's for sure—and **nothing** was expected from me. Kids just want to play, so I was honored to be their play partner."

Legacy Emanuel also had a healing garden for the use of the littlest patients, and this became a favorite place to go.

"There are two or three big, painted cement turtles for the kids to climb on out there. I'd often help them climb the turtle so the parent could catch a breath or simply enjoy watching their child interact with someone other than staff."

As parents got to know Joan, they began to trust her to stay with their children for short periods of time. "One time I was asked to sit with a child while her mom got a bite to eat. That was total enjoyment. The little one was in a crib, but I got to do the 'goofy kid talk' thing and loved it. I was once asked to sit with a child, rocking and reading to her, while her mom and dad had a consult with the doc," she says.

Receiving this level of acceptance began to change Joan. She was amazed that these parents were willing to trust her with their precious children. Sure, it might only be for 10 or 15 minutes, but that didn't matter. Joan, the woman who only a few short months ago had to be kept from running into traffic, was now allowed to stay with an ill child while the parents were out of the room. It made her wonder. Was she worth more than she realized? Could she have more to offer? Were there more places she could make a difference?

Joan Starts Talking

This need to make a difference, to do more, began to drive Joan. She believed that her miraculous recovery had left her with a call to serve others, and she felt ready. She knew she had something to share, but she didn't know how. She wasn't even sure what she wanted to say.

Then, in early 2002, a new opportunity dropped into her lap. Dr. Bruce called to ask Joan to speak on a panel for optometric students at Pacific University in Forest Grove, Ore. These students were coming to the end of their studies and now needed to determine if they would graduate or continue studying to become specialists. Dr. Bruce hoped that by listening to speakers such as Joan, who could share personal experiences of neurological injury and recovery with the help of vision therapy, he could encourage them to continue their education.

His request was simple. He wanted Joan to share how vision therapy had improved her life. Of course, Joan enthusiastically agreed. She couldn't wait for the chance to tell the students how this treatment put her world back together. "Dr. Bruce asking me to be a part of his TBI panel was by far the biggest compliment I could have been paid. I would be representing him and the 'magic' he does with his phenomenal work," she says.

She hung up the phone and began planning what she wanted to say. Joan had never talked in front of a group of people before and the idea of standing on a stage left her alternately excited and nervous. She still struggled with connecting what her brain wanted to say with the words that came out of her mouth.

"You have no idea how frustrating it is when you can't put sentences together to complete a thought," she says. She often found it challenging simply to remember what she was supposed to be talking about.

Although she no longer sounded quite like a drunk pirate, sometimes she would confuse words in a sentence, use a particular word out of context or make up an entirely new word. This often left whoever she was talking too baffled by the turn the conversation had taken. Now, Dr. Bruce wanted her to stand in front of a room full of people and try to express what she felt about him and his treatment. She knew it was going to be emotionally draining and worried she might make a fool of herself.

She decided to write down what she wanted to say on note cards she could read at the lectern. As she started practicing, she quickly ran into a problem. Each time she glanced up from her notes to look out at her pretend audience, she got dizzy. Her eyes couldn't process the motion between reading the small print on the cards and then looking into the distance to see the audience. Because falling over in the middle of her presentation wasn't an option, she created an enormous stack of note cards in a 22-point font. A few rounds of practicing her presentation in front of John and Shawn, and she was ready to go.

When the big day finally arrived, Joan, John, Shawn and Joan's sister Lisa piled into the car for the 40-minute drive to the university. They found their way to the auditorium, and Dr. Bruce introduced Joan to the three people who would join her on the panel. Then, with a few last-minute words of advice, Dr. Bruce told the anxious Joan that it was her turn to speak.

Joan was shaking as she looked out into the theater-style conference room where 50 students eagerly waited to hear what she had to say. In her best all-or-nothing fashion she believed these students would determine their future in vision therapy based entirely on *her* presentation. Not the entire panel; just her.

"I wanted to drive the point home to the students that this specialty was well worth it. They had the opportunity to either help hundreds with their optometry practice or touch thousands by adding behavioral optometry to their practices. My job, as I saw it, was to influence the students into making that choice."

Adding to her nervousness, Joan was emotionally invested in this opportunity on a completely personal level. This was her chance to do something for Dr. Bruce to thank him for giving her back her world, and she wanted to get it right.

"I wanted to make Dr. Bruce proud of me. He already was, I just didn't know how much."

She gathered up her courage, walked up to the podium, set out her stack of note cards and began to speak. She began with the crash and how it first led to RIO and then to Dr. Bruce. The students laughed as she recounted how she had tried to correct his treatment, insisting he was doing it wrong because of her previous work in the optical lab. Then she shared how the treatment changed her life and how grateful she was to Dr. Bruce. As she left the stage after her 10-minute presentation, she felt strangely exhilarated and wondered if she had gotten through to any of them. She didn't have to wait long to find out.

Several students approached Joan immediately afterward to thank her for sharing her experience. As they listened to her story, they realized they had options beyond doing routine eye exams. Her presentation made them realize they could offer a treatment that could change lives.

Their reactions were astonishing for Joan. "It was very humbling for me to be at the front of this class somewhat begging these kids to add the schooling for Vision Therapy so they could give hope to people who were in a situation similar to mine. There were quite a few kids that not only thanked me for sharing, they thanked me for helping them make up their minds and pursue their education."

Dr. Bruce took the speakers out to lunch to thank them and ask if they would be willing to join him again in the future. For Joan it was a no-brainer. She was hooked. Being on the panel that day had been even more enlightening for Joan than it had been for the students. Standing on the stage, recounting her story and seeing their responses unlocked something deep inside her. This wasn't just talking with others to make them smile. This was something different. Joan realized that by simply sharing her experiences, she could impact the decisions people were going to make about their futures. All she had to do was be herself and tell her story. It was overwhelming, exhilarating and more than a little bit scary.

Joan was so excited she could barely stand it. She couldn't wait to get into the world and see what else she could do.

The High Cost of Volunteering

John supported Joan's desire to change the world. At the same time he quickly realized the potential problems associated with Joan's newfound volunteering endeavors. He wasn't necessarily concerned about her ability to reach her goals. If the past year had taught him anything, it was that she could do whatever she set her mind to. Rather, he worried that the constant activity would be too much for her to physically handle.

Two years had passed since the crash. Joan's body and mind were still recovering, and she required a tremendous amount of rest. To stay healthy and continue on the road to recovery, Joan needed at least eight hours of sleep at night, along with morning and afternoon naps. That left her limited time to be out and about.

Not only did her ambitious schedule run the risk of upsetting that delicate balance, but Joan was clueless when it came to identifying the symptoms of fatigue.

"I still wasn't quite in tune with the amount of rest my body still needed," she says ruefully. "It's fairly easy for a brain injury survivor to over pace themselves, and I did just that. When I felt good in the moment, I'd keep going."

Shawn understood Joan's frustration and need to be out in the world. "No matter what your injury or affliction is, if you are home alone dealing with it, you are going to get depressed. You have to engage yourself before you can move on," Shawn says.

Shawn also knew Joan had unrealistic expectations of how much she could do. Joan wasn't about to be told that she had limits, and anyone who tried to tell her she did was looking for a fight. She wanted to be out doing things, not lying around on the couch sleeping the afternoon away.

"I knew I had to keep stimulating my brain," Joan says. "I need to engage with people."

The relationship between her behavior and her fatigue was obvious to everyone except Joan. Just like her days in RIO, if she didn't recognize it, it didn't exist. She couldn't see that when she was tired she became easily aggravated and would start arguments over the slightest thing. As she wandered from room to room, she forgot what she was doing, where she was going or why. Her balance, unreliable at best, became even worse as she walked into walls and stumbled over chairs. The muscles in her arms and hands would begin to fail, leading to dropped dishes and spilled drinks, which led to more anger and frustration, because she didn't understand why.

"I had no idea I needed that much rest," she says. "When I was dropping stuff or banging into walls or whatever, I would blame it on the damn brain injury instead of thinking to take care of myself."

She hated it when others insisted she needed rest and irrationally blamed John because he usually ended up as the one who pointed out her fatigue. Instead of accepting that his goal was to help her learn to take care of herself, she believed he was intentionally hindering her desire to get back into the world. She viewed his attempts to help her with her time management skills as intrusive, designed strictly to point out that she couldn't function as well as others could. In her eyes, John wanted to keep her home, to keep her safe and to treat her like a child.

"John was so lost when he had to tell me no, or tell me to slow down, only to have me come back and yell, 'Don't tell me that!' He always got the worst of it," Joan acknowledges.

Joan's refusal to accept his help was infuriating, but John knew he had to keep trying. As the silent witness to the results of the long days when she refused to rest, John suffered right along with her. Forced into a delicate dance of balancing the need to help Joan realize she needed to rest without pointing out her symptoms, John walked a constant tightrope. If he did it correctly, Joan would think napping was her idea and all would be well. If he were too insistent, he ended up bearing the brunt of Joan's anger.

"It was very frustrating," John says of Joan's refusal to rest. "It was obvious to me what was happening and why. I could point it out, very gingerly, but I'm not her boss. All I could do, really, was to attempt to be a guide and hope that eventually she would discover it on her own, because then it would stick."

"I know because of Joan's personality that she was not going to accept a command. And it was not my personality to give them. More often than not, rather than offering a suggestion, I would ask her a question. 'How do you feel?' or 'Are you tired?" John hoped that asking questions would lead Joan to a moment of self-discovery.

And it would, Joan says, "but it pissed me off, because I had been outed." Still she admired John's underhandedness. "He will never admit this, but he was so good at how he masterminded things. He made it my idea."

One memory that makes her giggle was how John used her guilty conscience against her to accomplish his goal of getting her to eat, even if she didn't want to.

"Dinner is ready," John would say.

"I'm not hungry," Joan would reply.

"Oh well. I made you dinner, but it's OK if you don't want to eat," John would say with a dramatic sigh.

"Now I feel bad," Joan would think. "He made me dinner, and I won't eat it. I don't want him to feel bad after he did all that work. I guess I should try something."

"OK, Husband, I'll try a little bit," she would offer.

"No, no, no," John would reply, shrugging his shoulders in defeat. "It's OK."

"Oh give it to me!" Joan would demand as she slammed herself into the dining room chair. She would eat the entire meal to make him feel better.

This, of course, was John's entire plan. He was shameless about using whatever tricks he could come up with to keep Joan healthy, and if a little guilt was necessary so be it.

"That wasn't difficult at all," John says. "It was just part of what you do." It was part of their new normal.

It would be months before Joan figured out the game. When she did, it shocked her to realize that everyone around her was in cahoots, twisting her reasoning around until she believed that she was the one making the decisions to take better care of herself.

"Oh my God, they knew me," she says.

Even though Joan had now been out of the hospital for two years, her loved ones still had to help protect her from herself. They had learned that living with a brain injury survivor meant never completely letting down their guard. They may not have had to be as hypervigilant as they had been in the early days after RIO, but the concern never went away. John, Shawn and the rest of the families were always aware of her. What was she doing? Where was she? Did she need them?

At the same time, they didn't want to hover. "When we're talking about constantly being on guard, the hardest part was finding the balance between letting her be independent and doing everything for her," explains Shawn. "I was still vigilant, but I tried to do it under the radar, because she needed to develop the skill and the confidence that she could do things by herself."

Frustrating as the process was, as time went on, Joan slowly began to accept the possibility of a relationship between actions and results. She started to identify the times a double shift at the flower cart led to broken dishes at home. She acknowledged that the days she had been in a fog at Pediatrics were the same days she had missed her morning nap. Intellectually, she began to make the connection between the need for rest and performance. Although it still irritated her, it slowly became more acceptable.

Learning to Rest

Joan was sure she didn't need rest, but when the opportunity came up for her to participate in a trial program to help others, she quickly agreed. This trial would use the television in her house as a way to send her reminders on how to take better care of herself using visual prompts. After discussing what kind of reminders she might need, her television was programmed to come on when it was time to rest.

This agreement turned out to be a decisive moment in her quest to understand her limitations. She went in thinking she was doing a favor by acting as a human guinea pig. She knew she didn't need something like this, but she was more than happy to test the program and provide feedback. She even agreed to curl up on the couch when directed so she could give a report about how it felt. She never expected it to work.

"I'd lie down, figuring I wasn't going to fall asleep, and lo and behold I would," she says.

Using these reminders allowed Joan to see for herself how taking those two naps each day could change how she felt in the evening. Instead of picking fights because she was overly tired, she could enjoy spending the evening with John, visiting, watching TV and relaxing. When rested, she could cook dinner without breaking plates or forgetting what ingredient came next in her favorite recipe.

"I finally knew why my body and mind were turning against me. It was doing what was necessary to keep me alive." she exclaimed.

Surprisingly, she also found that even if she gave in and took time to rest and care for herself, she could have an amazing day.

"It seemed like the days when I had to miss volunteering, something extraordinary would happen to me. I'd get a call from someone I hadn't heard from in years, I'd get called and asked to speak for an upcoming event somewhere, or I'd cook something spectacular for Husband for dinner."

Understanding that she could have balance in her life came as a revelation for Joan. Resting didn't mean giving up. It didn't take away from her day. It added to it. Finally realizing she could have the best of both worlds, she dedicated herself to being more careful in the future. This revelation also began to make her wonder why she had insisted on pushing herself so hard.

It would be many more months before Joan understood that much of her struggle came from her need to seem normal to those around her. Although she didn't think she had changed, she understood that she appeared different to everyone else. She felt she was letting them down, and it broke her heart.

She wanted to go back to the days of being Shawn's "Edith,"—not because it was important to her, but because it was important to Shawn. Even worse, she didn't want John to see her as someone different. She wanted him to have his Old Joan back almost as much as he did. Her desire to be normal, to push herself to do well, to achieve, was as much for his sake as for hers. She wanted him to have his world back.

She could see John's struggle to incorporate this New Joan into their old lives, and she wanted to help. She just didn't know what to do. Even John wasn't sure what to do to help him accept his new normal. Sure, he was saddened by the route his life had taken, and for what he and Joan had lost, but he knew his only option was to persevere. Joan was still his one true love, and there was nowhere else he wanted to be. Sometimes, though, the challenges were overwhelming.

"It can be very frustrating," he says. "You get constant shocks that will remind you. One of them was in October 1999. We went to the beach for the first time after the crash, and one evening, Joan was cooking spaghetti. How many times had she done this over the years? She got to the final step of putting the casserole dish into the oven and she couldn't figure out what to do. She just stood there crying." Watching her suffer, yet again, broke his heart.

Accepting this new reality came slowly. Sometimes John even struggled to remember that there was a reason behind Joan's odd behavior.

"Sometimes I could almost forget about the injury, and when I would see a certain behavior, I would just think, 'You're being obstinate' or whatever. We both have to constantly remind ourselves about what's going on."

Joan saw John suffering, and it left her with a tremendous amount of guilt. She would do anything to make him happy, but wondered if he really accepted her for who she was now rather than who she had been. She often believed she was fighting the ghost of Old Joan for her family's sake, even though deep down she knew she wasn't that person anymore.

She wanted John to see the same person she saw when she looked in the mirror. She didn't have an emotional connection with Old Joan, didn't really want to be Old Joan, and was frustrated that John couldn't accept her for who she was now. She wanted to move forward, but believed he was stuck in the past. Neither of them could figure out how to move on. Instead they constantly searched for something to provide a familiar link to their previous relationship.

Drinking Again

One night in 2002 Joan suggested that she and John share a beer. She may not have remembered the physical feelings associated with drinking, but she could remember sitting on the couch with John after work sharing beverages and talking about their day. Maybe recreating this picture would make him happy and rekindle their relationship? Could this be a starting point for moving on? It made sense for her because when Joan thought back to those early days, she saw a pretty picture in her mind of togetherness and enjoyment. John, on the other hand, wasn't so sure. He had been sober since the crash and when he remembered those days it brought back only memories of arguments and drama.

"She asked me frequently to go get some beer, and I said, 'No, that's not a good idea'," John says.

Despite his misgivings, John soon gave in to Joan's requests and stopped for a six-pack on his way home from work. The rush of alcohol was a balm to both of them. Alcohol helped dull the painful emotions they faced every day. Being drunk took the edge off, allowing them to forget their losses and the struggles they still faced. It helped numb the pain.

This reaction surprised no one. Alcohol and drug abuse are common side effects of traumatic brain injuries, according to Teresia Hazen from the Healing Gardens. Healthy coping skills are painful to learn and difficult to continue. Sometimes patients find it easier to self-medicate.

"So many of our clients come from drug backgrounds or alcohol backgrounds," she says, "Or they choose to use drugs or alcohol to cope with their TBI." John and Joan were no different.

Bonding over their nightly beverages, Joan and John conveniently forgot their past issues with alcoholism. They believed they had discovered a way to recreate their old lives, and it would be beneficial to their future. Before they knew it, they had fallen back into their old patterns. Dinner wasn't complete without some kind of alcoholic beverage, and weekends meant getting drunk. Stopping by the store for a six-pack on the weekend became downing a short case of beer every night. John and Joan were right back where they started, bringing Joan's recovery to a screeching halt.

"One thing to keep in mind is that they had both gone through so much," Shawn explains about their backward slide. "There had been pain and joy, and hurt and recovery, really high highs and really low lows in a short period of time, and that changes the way you think about things and the way you act on things."

As much as he had hoped that Joan was right and that alcohol would give them a path back to their old lives, after a year of trying John knew it wasn't working. Instead of a benefit, he saw the glaringly negative effects alcohol had on him, on Joan and on their relationship. With the acknowledgment of using alcohol to self-medicate came the disappointment of feeling drunk, hung over and out of control.

"I just finally decided this is not good, it has to stop," he says.

He knew it was time to quit. But how? His grand plan involved stopping cold turkey, but he was afraid he wouldn't be able to stick to it when times got rough.

Luckily, John had several friends who had successfully battled their own demons of alcohol and drug abuse, and he decided to turn to them for help. He arranged to meet with them as a group one night after work to stage his own intervention. Looking at his friends seated around the table John explained that he recognized the unhealthy and potentially destructive path he was traveling. He knew they had been successful and wanted to learn from them. He told them he needed their guidance and their support for what he should do next. Then he waited. Their answer was anticlimactic.

"They, said 'Stop!'" he says. "I came home and told Joan what I had done, and she was on board, just like that."

Joan easily agreed with John's decision. For her, alcohol was less about getting drunk and more about bonding with John. She knew that part of John's desire to drink came from a need to cope with his own demons. If drowning his emotions in alcohol made him feel better, she would drown right along with him. On the other hand, if he didn't want to drink, so be it. What mattered was helping John find a way to be happy.

"Because of all he had to go through in regard to the crash and my injury it wouldn't have mattered *what* I had to do in support of him," she says simply. Drinking, not drinking, it was all the same to her.

Then came the biggest epiphany of all. Once he sobered up, John realized he didn't necessarily want his old life back. The life he remembered, while good, was also filled with angst and alcohol, fear and anger. Now sober, John began to see that this new life, while still full of problems, had a different kind of potential. For the first time since the crash, he really looked at the New Joan. What he saw surprised him. This Joan was her own person, not a broken version of the Joan he remembered. This Joan was whole. This Joan was the woman he had fallen in love with all those years ago.

His New Joan didn't hide a lack of self-esteem behind booze. She wasn't afraid of how people saw her. She didn't worry about playing a role to make others happy. She was just Joan. She seized life with both hands and charged forward, stumbling all the way. This woman didn't consider herself broken. Sure, she knew she had some issues, but they didn't seem to be that big of a deal. All she wanted was to be happy, to make him happy and to make a difference in the world.

With this realization, John slowly came to see that he could be happy with Joan, even if she wasn't quite the person she had been. He could put his energy into moving forward with her instead of pining for the past. He could let go of some of his guilt over the accident and recognize that even though the changes to their lives were traumatic, they didn't have to define their world. He finally understood. While her injury would always complicate their lives, it was a life he was willing to embrace.

Not only did John's new mindset make him feel better, it helped relieve some of the pressure Joan was putting on herself. Her husband saw her for who she was and loved her anyway. She no longer had to fight a ghost from a past she could see but not feel. Finally, she could be New Joan. She could move forward and know that John was willing to come along with her. No longer stuck in the past, the time had come for John and Joan to see what the world had waiting for them.

The Birth of BIRRDsong

After three long years, things were finally improving for John and Joan. They were working as a team to build their new lives together. With John's alcohol abuse and longing for Old Joan now in the past, he could enjoy being with the Joan he had now. Joan spent her days speaking with Dr. Bruce and volunteering in Pediatrics and at the Flower Cart, while still dedicating herself to a routine that ensured she got enough rest. As she looked at her accomplishments, her driving need to make a difference was at least partially satisfied.

As she wandered through the hospitals, Joan was surprised by the interest she received from the doctors and students along the way. After all, not only had she had a miraculous recovery, she was someone who could articulate what it was like to live with a brain injury. Instead of dry, textbook examples or anecdotal stories from doctors, Joan could vocalize how it felt to be the patient. She could provide a firsthand look at what the patients of prospective ophthalmologists, optometrists and neurologists might be thinking and feeling during the recovery process. By offering this insight, Joan could help them become better doctors.

As she visited with staff and patients, Joan found she had could offer a similar benefit to those in RIO, and she found herself spending more and more time there. After all, she was one of them. She knew what it was like to have a brain injury. She understood their struggles and frustrations, because she had been there. She could relate to the feeling of being in a parallel universe where nothing made sense. She could sympathize with the depression that came with the never-ending insistence of everyone telling them they had changed.

Unlike the constant stream of doctors and therapists who wanted the patients to *do* something and family members who insisted they *be* someone they no longer knew, Joan accepted the patients for who they were right then and there. She was someone safe they could talk to about their problems and insecurities without fearing she would judge them. As a native speaker of this strange new world, Joan translated the rough spots and balanced out the traumas. She helped patients realize there was a life beyond the hospital waiting for them if they were brave enough to take that next step to get there.

Spreading her message to patients and professionals, Joan noticed another audience hanging on her every word: The families. These were the people who could do nothing but wait on the sidelines, just as Joan's loved ones had in those first horrible months. Often ignored, they spent hour after hour unnoticed as they sat next to the hospital beds, in the waiting rooms and at doctor's appointments. Waiting, watching, never sure of what would happen next, they lived in limbo as their spouse, child or friend fought to come back to life.

Joan realized her story brought hope to these lost souls, also. She knew, based on her own family's experiences, that they often felt forgotten in the hustle and bustle of doctors' visits and therapy treatments.

She started approaching the spouses and parents, letting them know she was available to talk about what she had gone through then and what her life was like now. By patiently answering their questions about the recovery process and listening to their concerns, Joan alleviated their fears. Through her, they found an understanding of what their loved one was experiencing and what they could do to help.

Joan loved sharing her insights but she also understood this place was nothing more than a short stop on a long journey. Physical, emotional and mental challenges didn't just go away once a patient checked out of the hospital. In reality, the recovery process could take years, and she knew how this would affect the entire family in ways they could not yet imagine.

Joan and John clearly remembered those first few months at home: how she couldn't use the bathroom by herself; how she would walk into walls because she didn't see them; how John could never let his guard down, because Joan might get hurt. Joan remembered how hard it had been to find her place in the world.

She knew how difficult it was going to be for these other families as they tried to incorporate the stranger who came home from the hospital back into their lives. Once they left RIO, she wondered, who could they turn to for help?

Joan had little faith in the few support groups that existed at the time. Those she had attended were run by well-meaning professionals who genuinely desired to help. The problem was that their only frame of reference came from textbooks and classes that gave advice on how to work with the brain injured. The leaders didn't understand what it felt like. Group discussions were built around accepting limitations rather than challenging survivors to move on to new experiences. The overall message was sympathy, rather than growth. Joan genuinely appreciated the effort the existing groups and their leaders were making, but it seemed to be off the mark. She wanted survivors to become empowered, not enabled.

"We had to start our own troubleshooting to find what works for us personally," she says.

That troubleshooting included addressing why the support groups never met in the same place, which left her scrambling to get from one end of town to the other. Why, she asked herself, couldn't there be a way to connect the professionals, the survivors and the families all in one location?

Adding to her frustration, Joan had issues with many of her fellow survivors. She wanted to be part of a support group that focused on improving her life, not learning to live as she was. She wanted to discuss her day-to-day challenges and get ideas on how to overcome them, not be told this was as good as it was going to get. She wanted to talk with people who were positive about their lives, people who had big plans for going forward. Instead, she found whiners who considered themselves victims rather than survivors.

"I was involved in a support group soon after the crash, but I dropped it because it was supposed to be support, but it was more like, 'Hi, my name is Bob, and this is all that's left of Bob.' And I was thinking, 'Crap, I don't need this," she complains. "They had no intention of moving on. They seemed to be complacent. They had accepted the idea that this was all that was left of them."

She was appalled when fellow survivors fussed that the world didn't change to fit them. "They complained about how nobody understood them and how angry that made them, and too many of them were intent on blaming everyone around them. I don't want anybody to fully understand me, because they'd have to have a brain injury in order to do so," she says, shaking her head in disgust.

Joan desperately wanted to find a better option. She felt encouragement was more important than venting, and she wanted to be around people who felt the same way. She wanted to spend time with people who believed in miracles and were grateful for second chances. She wanted to hear from those with personal experience in living with a brain injury without letting their injury define them. She was tired of listening to professionals. Joan knew like-minded survivors had to be out there somewhere, if she could only find them.

Providence struck once again. After seeing Joan's presentation with Dr. Bruce at the annual Brain Injury Association of Oregon Conference, a woman named Marih bounded up to the stage and shouted, "You kick butt, and I like you!"

Marih and Joan quickly found they had much in common. They were both brain injury survivors focused on moving forward rather than staying in the past. They were both happy in their new lives and eager to make the most of what they had. Marih, like Joan, found many of the support groups she attended discouraging rather than enlightening and Joan was ecstatic to discover she had an idea for change.

She wanted to create a support group that would be run by survivors for survivors—no more sitting through meetings led by those who didn't have a clue what it was like to be in their shoes. Marih envisioned a place where those with brain injuries could work together and learn from each other, empowering them all to move forward. Intrigued, Joan met Marih and her friend and fellow survivor, Pat Murray, for lunch a few days later to brainstorm.

Pat, also concerned about how the available support groups were run, was frustrated that each group seemed to focus on one thing. Some were for professionals, some were for women, and some addressed educational resources. Still others existed to talk only about holistic healing. This left survivors trying to coordinate which group they wanted to attend, at what location and at what time. It would have been confusing and time-consuming for someone without a brain injury. Instead, Pat envisioned a one-stop shopping approach, providing advocacy, mentoring, resources and friendship in one place.

"We decided we needed to address the needs of brain injury survivors and that survivors have to have some kind of say in this community," Pat explained as she described the perfect support group. "There has to be a place survivors can come, kind of like a big giant mentoring program."

Joan agreed, adding, "Because we are survivors, we know what works for us. We wanted to share the tricks that we have learned on our new journey to help make people successful. If a person was having a challenge, we wanted to offer a new way of trying something that had worked for us, in lifelike situations."

They envisioned an entity that would survive long into the future, providing everything from advocacy to social opportunities. Because no group like this currently existed, they decided to create it.

The determined threesome began researching different options and decided their best bet would be to establish a charitable organization, complete with tax-exempt status and a Board of Directors. They knew going in that it was going to be a tremendous amount of work, but they believed they were up to the job, brain injuries or no brain injuries.

"The biggest challenge was getting through all the legal stuff to become a 501c3," Joan remembers. "We had to write our bylaws, policies and procedures, file all kinds of documents and get a P.O. Box—lots of stuff that would be hard enough for a full-brained person to comprehend, so for we, 'the challenged ones,' it was tougher. Husband and Shawn did their best to explain things—and thank goodness for that."

"We started at absolute square one," Pat adds. "We had all these books on starting a nonprofit."

After hours of brainstorming around Pat's kitchen table, researching and reading, they found a helpful nonprofit attorney to get their paperwork ready to go. Now all they had to do was find a way to fund the cost of the legal fees associated with creating a nonprofit venture.

They decided to hold a garage sale to tell the world what they were up to and, hopefully, make enough to complete the process. Because of the large amount of donated items they collected from helpful friends and family, they held the sale in Joan's mom's backyard. On a rare sunny Saturday in Portland, they put up signs around the neighborhood explaining they were raising funds for a brain injury support group and waited for shoppers.

Joan was working the cash register when a couple came into the yard and stopped. They seemed a bit confused, so she asked if she could help them.

"The sign says this is for brain injury survivors," he replied. "Where are they?"

"You're looking at them."

"Oh," he said, confused.

As he walked away, Joan couldn't decide if she wanted to laugh or cry. "It was amazing. Were they expecting me to be drooling?"

At the same time she didn't feel insulted that he expected her to appear more disabled. "That is just people's ignorance and lack of education," she states bluntly. "They just didn't know. I think when people hear brain and injury in the same sentence, they think stumbling and drooling. They don't expect to see someone as high functioning as me."

Instead, she accepted his reaction as even more proof that she needed to show the world what a survivor of a brain injury could accomplish.

They only made about $500 that day, but they got their message out. People started talking about their plan, which led to enough donations to cover the cost of submitting their paperwork, and BIRRDsong was born.

"BIRRD is an acronym standing for Brain injury Information Referral & Resource Development," Joan explains. "The song part refers to a song, mantra, positive inspiration—however you want to phrase it—that a person holds in their heart to keep them moving forward. This is personal to each individual; however, everyone has one!"

"Sometimes, it's that song you have to call on to engage you to move your feet and keep walking with your head held high. The little jig may take you simply to a phone to call someone to help you overcome a disappointing situation or simply seek out positive interaction or words."

They had done it! They had their own group, created by survivors for survivors. An official entity, they could now reach out to those with brain injuries and their families to bring them out of isolation and into a world of support.

Moving Forward

In September, 2004, BIRRDsong was up and running. It was an answer to a prayer, but those first few months weren't easy. The mere existence of BIRRDsong should have been proof that those with brain injuries could move forward and accomplish great things. After all, it was a recognized nonprofit organization, complete with IRS status, a Board of Directors and a plan for the future. Unfortunately, they faced a constant struggle to get people to take them seriously. Their organization may have been the answer to a prayer for those with brain injuries, but many in the professional community questioned its reliability simply because it was run by the disabled.

Sadly, this turned out to be a common issue for those identified as having a brain injury, according to Pat.

"There is a preconception a person has in their mind of what a person is like with a brain injury," she says. "You can be very articulate, you can be doing a project together, but if they find out you have a brain injury, they start talking slower and louder. And you're going, 'Hello! I'm not an idiot.' I didn't automatically become intellectually challenged. I have a brain injury."

Complicating the fight against these preconceived notions was the fact that there were inherent problems in an organization run by those with neurological injuries. BIRRDsong was managed by strong-willed survivors determined to be successful. At the same time, the reality was that each also had some kind of intellectual or emotional impairment due to their brain injuries. Arguments, misunderstandings and hurt feelings were inevitable.

"In the beginning, we had to let a board member go because of hostility, and that wasn't too easy to do because of the brain injury mindset," Joan says. "However, this gal was getting way out of hand, and Marih simply told her it didn't seem to be a good mix and she'd probably do better for herself with a different group."

Additionally, not everyone appreciated the "stop your whining and move forward" attitude. Some simply preferred a more sympathetic environment and weren't ready for a more aggressive approach. Others wanted to vent, blame and complain, and they were resentful that their behavior wasn't going to be allowed. BIRRDsong was about moving forward, and its message was simple: Get on board, or get out.

Joan, in particular, was determined not to let destructive people derail the success of the organization she had worked so hard to help build. This was not a place to sit around, drink coffee and fuss about life with a brain injury. BIRRDsong was the place where survivors taught survivors how to be successful, how to get back into life, how to get back into the community. Its focus was on providing education, mentoring and examples of success and accomplishment. They were not about to let negative influences stop their mission.

"It's kind of like a transition," Pat explains. "They come into BIRRDsong, and they find out, yes, you have strengths. You are not just dealing with all the things you can't do. Instead, we ask, 'What do you have left? How do we build on it? What kind of support do you need?'"

Offering that support fulfilled another one of the missions Pat had envisioned. She finally had the one-stop shopping location she had dreamed of, where the community came to the injured instead of the other way around. Each month, BIRRDsong offered advice and guidance from a steady stream of professionals, including doctors, lawyers and social workers about their rights and responsibilities as survivors instead of disabled patients. Here they could interact with their fellow survivors, who could offer suggestions and help in living with a brain injury. They could learn that having a brain injury didn't mean losing an old life. It meant gaining a new one.

"So many times people had it drilled into their heads that they are not worth anything, that they can't rejoin the community," Joan explains.

She wanted to change that mindset. She wanted to show people how to leave their homes, leaving behind the stigma of being *damaged*. Joan understood that she was an anomaly and that not everyone would recover as she had, but that didn't mean they couldn't have a life. Even getting out of the house for a few hours could be an improvement.

"With the members of BIRRDsong and their families and friends, we can go out to the Japanese gardens, or we can go out to lunch and help them understand they are still a vital part of the community," she says.

The dream of helping others understand and come to terms with their injury was coming true. Survivors finally had a place they could go to find guidance on how to keep perspective about all of the changes in their lives. RIO gave them an understanding of the big things, like walking, talking and safety. BIRRDsong gave them an understanding of the little things. Things like losing the ability to vacuum the house easily.

"Because of my limited peripheral vision I am unable to see things downward as I'm looking straight ahead," Joan explains. "It happens every time I vacuum. I trip on the cord, because I can't see it, pull it from the wall via my feet, or I am unable to get the stupid thing to stand up if I had to lift it over anything."

"I've driven the damn thing into walls, vacuumed up throw rugs, change, socks, whatever I've failed to pick up off the floor before I started. I sometimes have to use just the tube or arm—whatever you call that thing—and have to be very careful I am only vacuuming stuff I intend to vacuum. Husband has always been willing to do it; however, I see it as a challenge that I will someday conquer without the colorful language that accompanies it."

Fellow survivors could have someone to talk to, to laugh with and to share the never-ending frustrations that come with brain injuries. Members could also find help with the life-changing moments still to come, when survivors just needed to talk to someone who had been through what was ahead.

"BIRRDsong is more of a personal support group, an eyeball to eyeball, social group. It's a very social, educational and holistic approach," Pat says.

By providing a safe place to interact with those living life and succeeding in spite of a brain injury, survivors would no longer have to suffer in uncertainty and fear, hiding in the shadows. Instead, this group was about encouraging, empowering and celebrating success, even if success meant only being brave enough to get out of the house and come to a brain injury celebration picnic. It helps survivors get back into the world.

"What society has done to people with a brain injury is to put them in a box," Joan explains. "What BIRRDsong did was to open the lid on the box."

"Through all the struggles, my greatest joy was when I saw people grow and achieve self-worth. That was my hot button with BIRRDsong—to help people not only to accept their disability but to give it positive power so it can help influence their lives and the lives of others, never playing down the challenges, but learning from them and aiding others with the wisdom from the lessons learned."

And there were so many lessons to share. Survivors had to accept that getting out of RIO and going home was only the beginning of their journey. There was often no end to the trauma of living with a brain injury. They may not get a happily ever after. They may never recover what they lost. Instead, they have a brand new life to learn to live. Joan, Pat and Marih wanted to be there for them. That means helping prepare them for what is to come, no matter how long it takes—preparing them to face the third year after the initial injury, for example.

"The third year is hell," Pat states. "The third year is when you hit the wall. Around the third year you have to come to terms with it, and it's hell, and there's that death and dying process of having to give up who you were, who you were professionally, what you were doing, the skills you don't have any more. Then you have to get back up.

"Later, around year four, it's like OK, this isn't going to change. This is the rest of my life. I'm probably not going back to work. I have to go get my Social Security Disability. What am I going to do with my life? And that's kind of the time when people start looking around and asking what is next."

"It's looking at yourself and saying 'OK, this is what I've got,'" Joan adds. "You have to come to terms. If you don't take ownership, you ain't going nowhere. You are just going to be going around in circles."

Helping people cope, helping them learn, helping them succeed, this was what they had dreamed of. Happy with their success so far, Joan, Marih and Pat wanted to keep going. They knew that during the drama and disaster of a brain injury the focus is on the person who is injured, but they were not the only victims.

"The survivor doesn't have to be the person who survived the injury," Joan remarks. "John was also a survivor."

They believed it was crucial that their organization offer support to the families as well, using the same model of "for survivors by survivors." This put John, usually quietly standing in the background, directly in the spotlight.

Through him, families learned how to cope with the changes in *their* lives. John understood that miracles come with a cost and that many people pay the price, not just the injured. He knew the pain of watching a loved one struggle through the recovery process, and he was willing to share how he survived. He talked about the horrible months of constantly watching Joan to make sure she didn't run in front of a car. He validated concerns about helping too much or not enough. He offered advice on how to come to terms with the reality, and fear, of discovering the person that came home from the hospital was not the same person who had been there before. In their own private group, John gave family members a safe place to vent, to say the things others might consider horrible or unloving, and to express their loneliness and anger.

He could even help give them perspective on survivor guilt. John easily admitted there were times in the beginning when he felt guilty about what had happened. After all, he was the one driving the car. He was the one who got lost, putting them directly in the path of the drunk driver. If he had only done something different when they first got hit, there would have been a different outcome. Then a random conversation helped him put the situation into perspective.

"While I blamed myself in some part because I was driving when we were hit, I learned that one of the witnesses told the police officer that when we got hit the first time the back of the car lifted up. That told me that it didn't matter what I did with the steering wheel because the car was out of control at that point. There was nothing I could do. And that helped me let go of the guilt."

"I also realized that no one knows what's going to happen or when and where. If it hadn't happened there, it could have happened on the way to work one morning. I can't allow myself to take overwhelming responsibility for it, because you have to move forward. It's just the way it is," he states flatly. It was often a tough message for the loved ones to hear, but it was one they often needed. It was part of accepting all of the aspects of life that could change after a brain injury.

If Joan was a beacon of hope for recovery, John was a beacon of hope for the future. Many of the husbands, wives and siblings had spent months hearing that their loved one was lost forever. The only guidance offered was that they needed to learn to cope with the myriad changes that were going to keep coming. John gave real life examples on reconnecting with a loved one from the position of someone who had been there.

During the family meetings, John described how he worked with his brain-injured wife to create something beautiful and new in their relationship rather than feeling condemned to the role of caregiver. He didn't sugar coat the struggles and pain they were facing and would continue to face. Instead, he offered hope that the struggles were going to be worth it.

Joan was ecstatic about John's willingness to be the spokesman for the families. She knew he would have preferred to stay in the background, but also knew how important it was that the families have a connection with someone. Joan had heard the stories about the divorce rate in couples with a brain-injured spouse. She knew the risks of the long-term stress and the effects it could have on a marriage.

John's willingness to speak at their events provided an opportunity to show a marriage could be saved and even grow stronger. By being the voice of the spouse who had been where they were, John could offer a connection to those facing the same issues, possibly making the difference between divorce and reconciliation.

Joan and John had seen firsthand how their story had affected and saved other marriages. In one instance, Joan met a man who had suffered a brain injury after driving drunk and crashing his car. At their first meeting, she saw a deeply depressed person whose marriage was rapidly falling apart.

"I told him about BIRRDsong and the fact I co-founded it and what we had to offer. Most of all, I mentioned the support and total understanding of his new journey. After a while, he and his wife came to a meeting, and they both got an understanding of the significance of his injury, how life gets rocked to the core and how, through support, life can and will go on. It's up to the persons affected to find their new place and to not let the injury define who they are."

"I introduced him to other members of BIRRDsong who were able to shed light on issues they were suffering with personally. From that one meeting they were able to see the crap they were going through was part of the steps, and it's up to them to use the tools we can provide to help them through."

"A marriage saved, along with sanity and new friendships evolved! Talk about touching lives! This was why I was blessed with this injury, and it was a prime example of what I envisioned at BIRRDsong's birth."

Joan was delighted by how this venture was turning out. She finally had a way to connect professionals in the community to those who needed them. She had answers for the patients and the families at RIO when they asked her what they should do next. She could offer help for the next stage of the journey where she and BIRRDsong would be waiting to guide and mentor other survivors. This was a dream come true.

A Lesson in Law: Part One

Thrilled by how far she had come, Joan and John were not out of the woods just yet. The previous two years had been exhausting both physically and mentally for both of them; the bills were piling up, and yet another huge shock waited around the corner.

For Joan, the events of June 12, 1999, were a perfect storm of events that should never have happened. No one disputed that the driver who hit them had been drinking at the bar on Hill Air Force Base, that he was visibly intoxicated and that he left the bar in a vehicle. After crashing into their car, he returned home, called 911 and turned himself in, admitting to the arresting officer, "I shouldn't have been driving, because I was drunk."

Joan later learned he had been prosecuted by the military, dishonorably discharged after being found guilty of drunk driving and hit and run, and required to pay the Millers $8 a month for two years as restitution. It seemed an extraordinarily lax punishment considering what it had cost them, but what punishment would have been enough? Even sending him to jail for the rest of his life would not have given Joan back her world. In Joan's opinion, no penance existed to make it right.

On some small level, Joan found herself sympathizing with him. Yes, he had chosen to drink and drive, and that was wrong, but he took responsibility for his decision and had paid the price.

"I don't hate him," Joan says. "He also lost everything. His career, everything."

For Joan, the bigger issue was why those at the bar kept serving him, even after they could see he was intoxicated. Why didn't they cut him off? Why didn't anyone try to stop him before he left the bar? Why didn't anyone at the bar call 9-1-1 after he left?

"They allowed him to stumble out of that NCO [non-commissioned officers] club, get into his car and drive off the base. He was visibly intoxicated, and no one stopped him. They robbed him of what could have been a promising military career."

These questions made sense to Joan because she is from Oregon, where businesses that serve alcohol have a responsibility to care about the results of overserving patrons. Often referred to as *dram shop laws*, these statutes basically state that if an employee of a bar serves someone visibly intoxicated, and that person harms someone, both the business and the server can be sued for damages along with the patron.

These laws were based on the idea that a person who has had too much to drink may be simply incapable of determining they are impaired. Designed to protect the community from those who cannot save themselves, dram shop laws require businesses that serve alcohol to take an active role by training their employees to watch for incapacitated patrons, stop serving them and call 911 if necessary. If they don't, they can be held responsible for a customer who harms someone while drunk.

Because of these laws, if Joan's crash had occurred in Oregon, she could have sued the bar to cover the medical bills that were quickly piling up. And they needed help with those bills. By the time it was all over, Joan and John owed more than $1,300,000 to various hospitals and medical facilities, including:

- Ambulance rides: $2,000
- Emergency brain surgery, four days in coma and two weeks in ICU: $1.2 million
- Jet from Ogden to Portland: $6,000
- Month in RIO: $60,000
- Assorted surgeries: over $21,000

Even with their insurance paying 95%, John and Joan still owed over $50,000, a bill they would slowly chip away at over the next 10 years, all because of the choices of a driver, a server and a bar owner. This seemed like a cut-and-dry case for a dram shop law.

To her surprise, Joan discovered this idea of holding bars responsible didn't apply throughout the United States. Each state prosecutes drunk drivers and deals with the damage they leave behind in its own way. Fortunately, Utah had a dram shop law that clearly stated that bars which served alcohol to someone obviously under the influence could be liable to a third-party for injuries and damages. Joan and John breathed a sigh of relief. The driver was drinking in a bar on Hill Air Force Base in Utah, and Utah had a dram shop law. In their minds, they should be able to expect the owner of the bar, their own government, to pay the rapidly rising medical bills just like any other bar owner who allowed their waiters to overserve someone who was obviously drunk.

It was not to be.

When Joan and John contacted an attorney to begin a lawsuit against the bar, they were told that because her crash involved a serviceman who had been drinking on a military base, dram shop laws didn't apply. To their amazement, they learned they would not be allowed to sue for damages because the base bar belonged to the U.S. government. They were stunned. How could this happen in America? Why were members of the U.S. military, and the bars that served them, getting away with injuring the very people they were supposed to protect?

Not going down willingly, John and Joan filed a lawsuit against the U.S. government, demanding an acknowledgment of what had occurred and compensation for damages. With their valiant lawyers, they fought for five long years, only to be told repeatedly they couldn't sue the federal government. Their case made it all the way to the Utah State Supreme Court where they finally lost once and for all. They were on their own.

"The military base was not held accountable, so we had no recourse but to pay for our own medical damages and loss of livelihood, because I can't work," Joan says, frustrated.

As Joan understood it, the U.S. government was hiding behind a grand conspiracy to prevent lawsuits against the bars on its bases. Under these rulings, someone injured by a drunk solider, airman, seaman or marine had no recourse. If the driver had been drinking off base, she could have sued. Because he was drinking on base, she couldn't. It didn't make sense.

The unfairness of the situation rocked Joan to the core. She wanted more than the driver punished. She wanted the government held responsible for the actions of its employees. This lack of accountability infuriated her. As far as she was concerned, this entire situation was wrong, wrong, wrong, and she was going to let anyone who would listen know that had been victimized by a government more interested in protecting itself than its citizens

"The military is sending loaded weapons off their bases disguised as drunk drivers, and we're all targets," she says.

Joan tried to make it clear that she didn't necessarily blame the members of the military who drank. Her issue was with the bars that let them keep drinking, refusing to protect them when they were obviously impaired. She was devastated for the airman who suffered for his bad decision-making simply because no one stepped in to stop him.

"They allowed this guy to be overserved—granted he was wrong for drinking—but once that alcohol hit the pre-frontal cortex of his brain, he lost the ability to make a good decision. They robbed him of a promising military career for the sake of a buck. Bull Crap! They changed lives. They ruined lives—all for the sake of a buck."

Joan had found a new message to share. Along with helping people recover from their brain injuries, she was going to make sure she spread the word about the double standard. She may have lost her fight against the feds, but she wasn't going down quietly.

She just needed to figure out how to get the word out to the world.

Joan and the VIP

Joan started by contacting the Oregon Chapter of Mothers Against Drunk Driving (MADD) to see if they had a place for her. After hearing her story, the director pointed Joan toward the Multnomah County Victim Impact Panels (VIPs).

These panels, found throughout Oregon, are part of the criminal justice diversion process for those charged with driving under the influence, who have not injured or killed anyone. By focusing on education and counseling rather than punishment, the diversion system allows a driver to avoid jail time by paying fines, undergoing an alcohol assessment and attending a series of classes, including a VIP.

VIPs offer an opportunity to hear from speakers who have been directly affected by a drunk driver. Families tell stories of lost loved ones, nurses and emergency services personnel talk about hopeless rescues, and survivors share how their lives were changed because of someone else's choice. Some of the most powerful stories come from drunk drivers reliving how they injured or killed someone because of their choice to drink and drive. For the first-time offender, a VIP offers a hard look at what could have been.

The VIP coordinator explained to Joan that the program follows a philosophy of treating an offender as someone who had made a grievous mistake, instead of as a criminal. Organizers hope that after hearing from those directly impacted by a drunk driver, offenders will think twice before making the same mistake again. Speakers are asked to assume the people in the audience are not bad, stupid or reckless. Instead, they should be viewed as good people who made an incredibly bad choice.

Learning about these panels and their philosophy lit a fire in Joan's heart. She would be able to tell people about the dangers of drunk driving and the added risks associated with being hit by someone in the military in one presentation.

Excited, Joan wanted to sign up to speak that very night. The VIP coordinator, however, advised a more cautious route. She knew that sharing a personal story about being the victim of someone else's poor decisions could be unexpectedly traumatic for survivors. Joan might think she knew what she was getting into, but the coordinator wanted to be sure she understood what would happen when she got up on stage. She asked Joan and John both to attend several presentations to help them decide whether Joan was emotionally ready for the impact of speaking out.

Readily agreeing to these conditions, Joan and John made arrangements to attend their first presentation the next week. Arriving at the auditorium, they received their first shock of the night.

"There must have been 150 people there, all charged with drunk driving," Joan says. "It was presided over by a judge, with security in the room, and taken very seriously. There were ground rules right off the bat, like no wearing of hats, no drinking or eating, no talking, no gum chewing. If they had to go to the bathroom, it was 'go now,' because they're not allowed out of their seats once the program started."

It was a wake-up call for both of them. Until that day they believed their situation was an isolated case, and Joan would be speaking to a small group. They simply had no idea there were so many drunk drivers on the roads of America. And those were only the ones who had been caught. Who knew how many others were out there, sneaking by police officers and barely making it home each night?

"It gave us a whole new outlook on other drivers," John says.

Once the presentation started, Joan and John began to understand why the VIP coordinator was so adamant they listen before Joan spoke. Attending the panel was as overwhelming as she had warned them it would be, which caught them by surprise. After all, they helped create BIRRDsong to help people cope with the trauma of life-changing events. They knew how to talk to victims and what was needed to help them move forward. Adding the VIP to their repertoire should have been easy.

There was just one small problem. At BIRRDsong, they had the answers. They were the ones that others came to hear. They were in control.

Here at the VIP, they were the ones listening—listening to what it was like to no longer be in control because of someone else; what it was like to be damaged because of the poor choice of another person; what it was like to be a victim; what it was like to be them. It rocked their world. For the first time, John and Joan heard their lives described by someone who could feel what they felt. The anger. The despair. The loss.

Attending the VIP was both cathartic and draining. John and Joan found a sense of relief, realizing they were not alone. There were others out there just like them, people who could relate to what they were going through, who they could talk to and share their struggles with. It was like BIRRDsong for the victims of drunk drivers.

Then it hit her. As she looked around the room, Joan suddenly realized it wasn't just the people *on* stage she could relate to. To her shame, she saw herself reflected in the faces of the crowd. These people, who could have killed someone because of their alcohol use, were just like Old Joan. These were people who had made a bad choice in life, just like she had done so many times before. These were people someone could have stopped, but didn't.

Joan sat in that audience and thought about the many times she had driven drunk without getting caught. She remembered running through the rain with a pillow over her head after her hit-and-run as a teenager. She thought about the damage alcohol had done to Old Joan, and she wondered how she had gotten lucky enough to have never ended up sitting in an audience like the one in this room.

Joan struggled against tears as she watched the faces of those in the audience. Some cried; some hung their heads in shame; some refused to make eye contact with anyone else. Still others seemed annoyed they were there, refusing to admit they had done anything wrong or that they might have a problem with alcohol.

Sitting at her side, John was also stunned by the realization that it could have been them sentenced to sit in the audience as offenders rather than visiting as a potential speaker. He spent that first presentation thinking back on the mistakes he and Joan had made.

"We've all done it," he says, "and we all learn in our own way and in our own time, and that is unfortunate. It can have disastrous consequences."

"The meeting definitely did what it was supposed to, which was impact us," Joan says, remembering the emotions that flooded them.

Joan and John attended several presentations before Joan felt ready to schedule her first appearance. With Shawn along for moral support, John drove Joan to the venue. She checked in with the VIP coordinator, who introduced her to the other panelists, and nervously waited for her turn to speak. When they called Joan's name, John helped her up to the steps to the stage, and she shakily approached the podium.

Dressed in a white *Touched by an Angel* sweatshirt, she opened her presentation by telling the audience that she was, indeed, touched by an angel, and that was the only reason she was still here on Earth. She then burst into tears as she struggled to describe the crash and her resulting injuries.

"I started crying and had a hard time going on," Joan says. She sobbed as she described what her life had become since that dreadful night in Utah and the unfairness of the double standard she had dedicated herself to fighting against.

Ten minutes later her time was up, and she left the stage exhausted. "I was totally spent," she remembers, and she couldn't wait to do it again.

The Speaker

Joan knew she had a powerful story, and she wanted to reach as many people as possible. She also knew it was going to be tough. She may have been full of enthusiasm, but it was incredibly difficult for her to get up on that stage and talk about her situation. Opening her heart and reliving all she had been through was often overwhelming and emotionally draining, which meant she struggled to stay on track.

"What I shared for quite a few panels was short and to the point, and I always cried. I always wore that sweatshirt, opened with the same line and then lost it," she remembers.

Plus, Joan was obsessed by the idea that she could use the Victim Impact Panels as a way to make people understand the risks faced by innocent citizens around the nation at the hands of the people who were supposed to be protecting them.

"I was gung-ho on exposing the military for not taking responsibility for sending loaded weapons off the base. The entire reason I was there was I wanted get the word out to expose the military."

To her surprise, that wasn't the message people were getting, and their reactions baffled her. She was trying to tell the story of how she had been wronged, but they were hearing a story of survival, love and second chances. Joan was amazed at how many people came to her afterward to thank her for sharing her story, and tearfully tell her how overcome they were by her presentation and how sorry they were for their own behavior.

Their reactions filled Joan with a strange mix of both sorrow and pride. She had no idea that hearing about what happened to her forced them to face their own mistakes. She was completely unaware that she was providing a huge benefit to their futures. She was proud she was helping, but sad about the obvious pain so many of the attendees were feeling. She didn't want to hurt them. She wanted to warn them about treachery.

More surprising was the number of times members of the audience approached John after one of her presentations. Unlike Joan, John didn't want the spotlight or the podium. He believed his job was to support Joan in *her* mission. He was perfectly content to sit in the back of the room while she shared from the stage. Sure, he spoke at BIRRDsong, but that was different. That was just chatting with families around a table, not standing at a podium addressing an audience.

The VIP was different. Whether he liked it or not, his love was an integral part of Joan's survival, and she was going to make sure everyone knew about her faithful and dedicated husband. Joan laughed at John's discomfort whenever she pointed him out in the crowd.

"I'd be on stage and say, 'I love you honey,' and people would look back at him and clap," Joan giggles.

"Every once in a while when Joan was speaking, she would say something that embarrassed me," John says. "People came up to me after, and they called me a hero and blah, blah, blah, and as far as I'm concerned, it was what you do. If you say you love someone, then this is how you acted, this is how you responded. You didn't just walk away. You acted like you love them. It was that simple for me."

"Men came up to him after I spoke and said, 'Thank you for showing me how a man acts,'" Joan says proudly.

John blushes. "That's when I wanted to go hide under the stairwell," he says.

Joan's main mission may have been to educate people to the double standard, but Joan never missed a chance for a shout-out to her husband. She knew in her heart that his love was a huge part of why she recovered, and she wanted everyone else to know it also. She also wanted to acknowledge how much he had suffered because someone else made the choice to drink and drive.

"I don't know if I ever said why I call Husband, 'Husband' and not John," she says one day. "After we were married, I was over-the-top happy that I had found a man who I truly loved for all the right reasons and who loved me for me. I hadn't experienced that before, not that it was any man's fault. However, John was able to find and catch the core of Joan and free that injured bird."

"Calling him 'Husband' was a constant reminder of how blessed I am that he stood beside me through so much change that was necessary for my health and sanity and life changes that came as a result of a bad choice by a young man on June, 12, 1999."

Joan was happy her presentation brought kudos for John, and acknowledgments about her recovery, but she was a little confused about why. What was she doing wrong that people were responding to how great John was instead of how horrible the double standard was? She didn't want people feeling sorry for her or telling her how they admired her. She wanted to get them riled up against injustice, and instead they wanted to praise her recovery. It was annoying.

Joan knew she was capable of choosing a message and getting it across because she had already done it with BIRRDsong. Her goal had been to educate people about brain injuries, and she did. Now she had a new message, about the double standard and the "loaded weapons," and she had a great new venue to talk in. It should have been working, and it wasn't. Something was missing.

It seemed like when she got to the part about the double standard, people patted her on the head and then went right back to talking about her miraculous survival and John's role as a husband. She didn't understand why her true message was getting lost.

Joan simply had too much to say. She wanted to discuss the double standard they had fought against, but she also wanted to talk about the dangers of drunk driving, her difficult recovery, how much she appreciated the staff at RIO, her experiences with BIRRDsong, her love for Dr. Bruce's Vision Therapy and her incredible husband, all in less than 10 minutes. Listening to her was like trying to chase a hummingbird around the room. Look one way, and it was here; look another, and it was there.

Adding to the challenge, Joan brought up her anger at the people who didn't stop the drunk driver from leaving the base, but not her anger with the driver himself. This was confusing for the audience, made up of people who were there to take personal responsibility for their choice to drink and drive.

Then there was the problem with her presentation style. Joan may have been a 40-year-old woman on the outside, but she often behaved more like a 5-year-old. She no longer had the life experience necessary to connect with a group of adults, and that came across in her presentations. Instead of appearing as a passionate adult with an important message, she overwhelmed the audience as a temperamental child who stomped her feet and demanded to be heard. She rattled from one topic to another, sure that she was on the right track, and then became angry when she didn't get her message across the way she planned.

Joan wanted to connect with her emotions in a way others could relate to so she could get her message across. She didn't want to be confusing. She wanted to be powerful! She needed to create a presentation that would be both meaningful and professional, but she didn't know where to start. She needed to find someone she could trust to help her connect what she wanted to say into one message that was easily understandable. Luckily, an old friend was waiting in the wings.

The Return of Kathy

For Joan, thinking about the past was like looking at someone else's photo album. She could see the pictures, but had no emotional memory attached to them. She knew she had been a cheerleader and could see the experience in her mind. It just didn't resonate as something she had done. There was no nostalgia or enjoyment when she remembered those days. It was just a fact, like algebra.

Even her memories of John suffered. While she could remember their wedding, she had no idea how it felt. There was no excitement of walking down the aisle or thrill of saying her vows. Instead, she saw a pretty picture that might have belonged to anyone. Losing the emotional connection meant she didn't feel she had lived the experience. It belonged to someone else. Everything from before felt muted and unreal, not attached to the life she was now living.

Those closest to her accepted those lost connections as a fact of life. They understood she wasn't intentionally shutting them out, and they worked to create new memories that could truly belong to her. It was the others, those who weren't part of her day-to-day recovery, who found it difficult to relate to New Joan.

When she ran into people from high school and didn't know who they were, she had to stop and explain her injuries. To her surprise, this often made others uncomfortable because they simply couldn't cope with what had happened. They would see the physical changes, the tottering walk, wacky eyes and shaved head and just stare and stutter. This hurt more than she could say.

"I loved when I bumped into these so-called friends and their lame excuse for not calling was they didn't know what to say," she says sarcastically. "I took that as 'you're different now, and I'm nervous about being around you.' Maybe that wasn't true, but that's how it made me feel. Crap, these *friends* didn't even bother to call my family after the crash to see how I was or if there was anything they might do."

Joan found it even more difficult to accept how those who could get past the physical challenges seemed stymied by the personality ones. Somewhere along the line, this new, confident Joan left the party girl they had known behind, and they didn't understand. That she was content, even in the face of all her challenges, confused them. Instead of being happy for her ability to adapt to a new life, they found her situation odd. They wanted the Joan they knew, the one they were familiar with, not a stranger.

Painful as it was to grasp the concept that people she had once considered friends no longer wanted to be a part of her life, Joan moved on. Her focus was on creating new memories, not worrying about old ones. If these people couldn't handle who she was now, so be it. She was done worrying about the past.

The past, however, wasn't quite done with Joan. At her father's funeral, she looked up and saw her childhood friend Kathy for the first time since that disastrous high school reunion years before. It was like a spotlight suddenly shining in a dark room that had been lit only by a night light. In that instant, memories and feelings of their friendship flooded her mind. Laughing together, playing as children, the excitement of being friends, it was all there.

"Kathy is the same Kathy I knew when I was growing up," Joan says.

"I felt like I was Oprah," Kathy says as she recounts hearing Joan scream her name from across the cemetery. She immediately knew that this person rushing toward her was not the same self-destructive Joan she had seen at the reunion. Then, Joan had seemed hopeless, an alcoholic and drug abuser who was simply surviving. This new version of Joan stumbling across the grass and giggling reminded Kathy of the friend she lost in high school.

When Kathy got home that night, she couldn't stop thinking about their chance reunion. She had attended the funeral out of respect to a family she had known for years. She never expected to reunite with Joan, much less find herself talking to a completely different version of the person she remembered.

"I knew Joan had been in an accident," she says, "But I had no idea how serious it was."

Although shocked at her old friend's physical condition, what surprised Kathy more was the energy and genuine enthusiasm for life Joan projected. This Joan, filled with love and laughter in spite of her physical and mental challenges, was the Joan who had disappeared at age 14, sucked into a life of alcohol, drugs, abusive relationships and crime. This was Kathy's Joan.

Determined to reconnect with her old friend, Kathy picked up the phone and called her that night. "I couldn't stay away from her," she says. "So I called her. I couldn't let it drop, even though 30 years had gone by."

Joan was overjoyed when Kathy called. Kathy may have just been touching base with an old friend, but for Joan the call led to the discovery of a treasure trove of memories and emotions. By some odd twist of fate, Kathy turned out to be a safe deposit box of Joan's previous life. In Kathy, Joan found an emotional link to the past, whether it was laughing while playing with Barbies as children or the fun-filled days of high school before everything went wrong.

"I can go back to Kathy to get whatever I need, because she has so much of my life. She holds onto my memories." Joan said.

Kathy felt humbled, and a bit awed, at finding out she carried Joan's emotional history. She wasn't sure she was ready to take on the responsibility of helping Joan find a future by providing a link to the emotions of her past. She had once stood helplessly by as Joan tried her best to destroy herself, and now she found herself as the key to all those memories. Would Joan really want them back? Would remembering the pain of the past hurt or help?

At the same time, Kathy believed that nothing happened without a reason. As she listened to Joan tell her story, heard her talk about her mission and her plans for her new life, Kathy knew she was meant to be involved. A firm believer in second chances, Kathy knew she was seeing a miracle at work. As far as she was concerned, the crash was sad, but necessary. It was an event that ultimately saved her old friend.

"Your true self has always been there," she tearfully said to Joan. "It was the alcohol and drugs and life situations clouding the water."

"Joan finally got the knock on the head she needed so she could become the person she was meant to be," Kathy says. "Her true self, her passionate self, has come back online after 30 plus years with a mission and passion of helping other people not to have to go through what she has gone through."

Kathy and Carolyn Have a Project

Intrigued by Joan's sense of a mission, Kathy wondered what else she could do to help. Little did she know that the act of picking up the phone that fateful day just to say hello would be the answer to Joan's prayer.

Kathy was a grade school English teacher who had found her soul mate in Carolyn Martin. Carolyn is a public speaker, keynote presenter and management trainer. They were the perfect team to help Joan improve her public speaking and presentation skills.

Eager to help, Kathy and Carolyn invited Joan to their house to show off her 10-minute VIP presentation. To their shock, Joan smashed and banged her way into the kitchen dragging her helmet, her walker, a photo album filled with pictures of her life since the crash and, strangely enough, her pompoms. Taking a deep breath, Joan ran through her presentation and anxiously waited for their input.

"Joan had so much energy, and she had so much to say," Carolyn says diplomatically. "But she couldn't stay focused. She had stories, and they were all over the place. She needed a script she would be wedded to, so the presentation would be logical, flow and be enticing and exciting to the audience."

Kathy laughed when she saw the pompoms in Joan's hands. Instead of bringing up memories of what was lost, Kathy saw them as a message about who Joan would one day become. "The pompoms are a symbol of your winning spirit," Kathy told Joan. "They became a symbol of holding onto something old, but letting something new blossom."

Kathy went to work creating a script to keep Joan on focus, no small feat for a speaker with so much to say. Joan's goal was to talk to anyone who would stand still long enough to listen, so Kathy needed to develop a one-size-fits-all presentation that would be easy for Joan to follow, while still including enough information to entice a variety of people to learn more. It had to incorporate all the points Joan wanted to make, from the military double standard, to the dangers of drinking and driving, to her love for John. It was a challenging project Kathy was more than happy to take on, if it would help Joan succeed in her mission.

In the meantime, Carolyn began working with Joan on her presentation skills and stage presence. She began the process by carefully explaining that Joan didn't need to drag all of her props onto the stage with her. She helped Joan understand that although each individual item came with a powerful message, the message was lost if she tried too hard. She and Joan worked together to determine which props would be most effective and when to use them to create the greatest impact. She then taught Joan how to embrace her strengths and worry less about her weaknesses.

"Carolyn explained the importance of being myself and talking from my heart and not my head," Joan says. "If I screwed something up, I needed to just keep going because no one would know the difference. Most important was to let my passion show. It was okay to cry, sweat or whatever. All these things just verified the journey I was on and my passion for change."

Joan may have wanted their help, but that didn't mean she was going to make it easy for them. With her undeveloped emotional skills, Joan could be a trial for the two women as they tried to explain what they were changing and why. She often argued, saying they "Just didn't understand what I was trying to accomplish."

In spite of Joan's defiance and reluctance to change, Kathy and Carolyn finally got her to cooperate long enough to create a scripted performance with limited props. Then they patiently watched while she practiced over and over until she could present her message smoothly and, for Joan, succinctly. Finally, they pronounced her presentation as complete.

"She was ready to take the show on the road," Carolyn says.

Joan had her message, her VIP audience, her script and her props. Thanks to Carolyn and Kathy, she felt confident in her ability to talk in front of a crowd. She felt successful, and as she stood at the podium looking at the faces around her, she realized she wanted to do even more. She wanted to connect with these people, both on the stage and off, on a more personal level. Joan knew she had survived for a reason. She knew she was supposed to do something. But what? How could she move to the next level? The answer would surprise her.

Joan Finds a Purpose

After all she had accomplished, what possibly could come next? Joan knew in her heart that she had survived for a reason. She had shown herself that if she put her mind to it she could build something great. BIRRDsong was up and running as a place where she could use her knowledge and experiences to help people heal. With Kathy and Carolyn's help, she was more effective when she spoke at the monthly VIP.

It still wasn't enough. She may have been happy with what she had accomplished, but it didn't fill her need to do more. She wanted to take what she had learned and create a plan that would educate the world about the military double standard.

"My biggest focus was that we had to do something to change the law," she says.

Dedicated to her mission, desperate to ensure no military bar let a drunk driver out the door again, she didn't believe she was accomplishing anything when it came to educating the public about her lawsuit. She felt like she was drifting down a river hollering at the banks hoping someone would hear her, and no one did. Joan knew she was capable of more, even with a brain injury. She just needed to get pointed in the right direction. But how? Once again, Providence stepped in.

In August 2008, John and Joan flew to Arizona to hear motivational speaker Chuck Goetschel speak at a business conference. They had been fans of Chuck's work for years and enjoyed listening to his messages of motivation and hope. He was one of the speakers they had hoped to hear at the conference they were attending in Utah the weekend of the crash. Now, almost 10 years later, they would finally have their chance to see him in person, and they couldn't wait.

"We respected what he talked about," Joan says. "He was very spiritual, and that was something that really appealed to me. God is very important in his life, and Christianity is his foundation."

Even as a lapsed Catholic, Joan still considered Christianity an important part of her life, and she appreciated that Chuck's message matched her beliefs. Those beliefs had become even stronger after an experience she had while in her coma.

"In the coma, I saw this fluffiness, not clouds or anything, but a billowy texture. There was a gate, not a pearly gate, but just a gate and a little girl sitting cross legged wearing a big straw hat shaking her head 'no.' I knew this messenger was my niece Brittany, who died of SIDS at seven weeks old. She was at the age she would have been now, 12 years old, shaking her head and saying, 'No Auntie Joanie.' She had grown up in heaven and was wearing a white dress, which just happens to be the same color of the one she was buried in."

For Joan, this *meeting* provided a clear message that her time had not yet come, and she needed to come back and begin again.

"My room wasn't ready and the wings didn't fit, so I had to come back and make a difference," she says.

"I already had those beliefs in my core before the crash, and after seeing Brittany in my out-of-body experience in the clouds, I knew this was my foundation. Listening to Chuck's message over the years strengthened my beliefs by helping bring me clarity about what I believed."

Reading and listening to his teaching also resonated with Joan, because it revolved around using faith to overcome adversity. Using examples from his personal life, he described how he had once lost everything and how he had recovered. In his heart-wrenching stories of struggle and recovery Joan found someone she could truly relate to. Like her, he had once had to start all over with nothing.

"It was something I could identify with because it was real," she says. "There was an honesty about him that rang so true when he talked about not knowing what direction to go."

Joan loved listening to Chuck's lessons about how having faith could make her strong enough to handle anything that came her way.

"He taught about having faith in yourself and faith in the Lord. His message was that if you weren't strong enough to handle the struggles, you wouldn't have been given the struggles."

This message hit home with Joan. Although she had stopped questioning why her life had taken such a negative turn, she still sometimes wondered why she and John had to suffer. Chuck's teachings helped her understand her part in a bigger picture and that God had created her to be just who she was. Through Chuck, she came to believe that God wouldn't give her more than she could handle.

"It was about *individualness*, being who you are, never trying to be anybody other than who you are, because God created you for you. Listening to Chuck validated what I had to go through because of my strength in God. I even challenged Him to bring on more!"

In addition to the message of faith, Chuck boasted a positive can-do attitude that thrilled Joan. Still surrounded by people who worried about her, forever reminding her to be careful, Joan loved hearing from someone who could teach her to look at the lighter side of life.

"I liked his voice. I liked his positiveness. I liked his affirmations and his spiritual and faith connections. It was refreshing. He could say the same thing over and over again, and I would still listen."

Now she was about to see the man she respected and admired in person for the first time, and Joan was a little concerned about what she would find. Chuck had given her so much hope during her darkest days. What if he turned out to be a fake? What if he didn't come across as honestly in person as he did on tape? What if he was in it for the money rather than to provide a message of hope? What if, when she finally saw him, he wasn't the person she wanted him to be?

Joan anxiously walked into the auditorium and took her seat. When he walked out onto the stage, she burst into tears. Chuck looked exactly as she had hoped.

"It was his aura," she says.

As he began his presentation on building a dream, following a passion and finding a purpose, his message rocked Joan's world to the core.

"That day is a blur, except for the part where he talked about finding a purpose. I had never thought about being someone with a purpose. I know we are all here on Earth with a job to do, but I never associated that with a purpose. It was an 'aha' moment. Realizing that the reason I'm here, all this speaking that I want to do is my purpose. It's not just something I wanted to do. It's why I'm here. To make a difference."

Joan knew she had a drive and a mission to tell her story. She had just never connected the desire to share her experiences to the reason she had survived the crash. Hearing Chuck speak about passion and purpose as parts of a bigger picture put an entirely new spin on her belief system.

"The passion is following what I want to do; the purpose is why I'm here on Earth. This is why God put me here. It's why I had to go through so much shit, because I'm strong enough to deal with it. So now I can even have more passion to follow my purpose," she says.

"It was on that day, I had a mental mind switch, an awakening—whatever you want to call it—and realized that my purpose was to teach, warn, influence, change people's thinking about how they viewed drinking and driving. If nothing else, I need to do my best to prevent what happened to Husband and me from happening to anyone else—to let people know they have a choice in everything they do, and along with choice, there are always consequences. So choose wisely, because all choices affect people around you. For the good or for bad, others are always affected."

It was almost more than she could absorb. For years, she had been listening to this man tell her that if she had faith she could be someone more than who she was. To succeed, she needed to believe that God had chosen her, had created her to be strong and had made her the person she was. This was the day she finally understood what he had been saying all along. She had a purpose.

Joan desperately wanted to stay after the presentation to talk to this man who had so suddenly changed her life. As she headed for the stage, she saw the long line of people with the same idea already waiting for their chance to talk to him. She and John had a flight to catch and had no time to spare for standing in line. Disappointed, they left the conference center and headed for the airport.

The minute they got to their gate, she sat down to create her plan. Excited about what she had discovered, she immediately pulled a notebook out of her bag and began writing out a list of people she could share her newfound purpose with.

"I had no idea what I was going to say," she says. "I just knew I wanted to talk about my purpose."

As she sat scribbling, once again Providence stepped in. She looked up to see Chuck waiting nearby for his flight home. "I was like a goofy rock star groupie," Joan says as she describes rushing over to share what she had learned from him.

"My purpose is to make people aware of the gift of choice and that everything that they do revolves around choice," she shouted at him.

As she babbled on, Chuck patiently listened to what she had to say and then encouraged her to go out and share with the world. To Joan's delight, he told her he was intrigued by her story and offered his e-mail and phone number so he could continue to provide advice and encouragement.

Boarding the plane, Joan reflected on what she had learned on that exhausting, exhilarating day. She felt like she had been wearing blinders that had suddenly been removed, leaving a whole new world filled not just with passion, but with purpose.

"The day I heard Chuck speak jump-started my passion because I discovered my purpose," Joan says. "I'd never seen it that way before. Up until then, the speaking was just something I was going to do, but now my heart was on fire! It was as though Chuck put a lasso around me, my thoughts, dreams and desires, then pointed me in the direction of my purpose."

Joan had put it all together and was off to change the world—just as soon as she figured out how.

Susan

Joan returned from Arizona filled with excitement and a new clarity. Thanks to Chuck Goetschel, she understood that when passion met mission it led to purpose. Now what? Not surprisingly, shortly after returning to Portland the answer found her.

It was 2008, and Susan Lehr had recently taken over as the director of Oregon Impact, an organization focused on providing educational experiences to end impaired and distracted driving. "We want to put ourselves out of business, basically," she says, describing the organization's mission.

As the new director, Susan wanted to broaden the VIP panel message with additional speakers and expand the organization's educational opportunities in the community, local schools and media. To get started, she was seeking a more diverse base of stories from people affected by impaired drivers. Shortly after moving into her office, she came across Joan's name and number and called her to see if she would be willing to chat. Joan jumped at the chance.

"I was familiar with Oregon Impact from my work with Multnomah County, so that was a no-brainer," Joan says. "But when Susan mentioned going into schools I was like, Holy Cow, Yeah! I had gone through the college thing with Dr. Bruce, but that was for optical students. Now I had the opportunity to go into schools and start educating them before they are sitting in the audience at a VIP. So it's proactive, preventive."

Susan was also excited about their upcoming meeting. After hearing the short version of Joan's story during that initial phone call, she knew Joan might be the person to fill a perspective missing on the panel.

"I knew that as a victim, Joan could talk about the experiences she went through," Susan says. "She could add a lot of value to the message if her presentation was good."

They met one afternoon for coffee and by the end of their conversation Susan knew Joan's experience would be a perfect fit for the panel. Her story of the military double standard was intriguing, but Susan saw even more in Joan. She saw someone unique, someone who could speak to both sides of the impaired driving concern.

If Susan was excited about adding Joan to her program, Joan was overjoyed by this new speaking opportunity. It had been five years since she had first enlisted Kathy and Carolyn's help to become a more effective public speaker. With their guidance, she had gained a new confidence in her own abilities to convey her message, but there was something lacking. Month after month, as she stood at the VIP podium reading from her script, she wondered if anyone out there really heard what she had to say. Even talking with all the people who came to her afterward to thank her for sharing her story didn't convince her that her message was making an impact. She worried that she would have the same problems when she started talking about prevention and choices.

"Prior to meeting Susan, I had gone to several presentations to speak and I couldn't understand why no one was asking me back," Joan remembered.

Joan was unaware of the differences between her presentations. When she spoke for the optometric students, she gushed about how wonderful Dr. Bruce was as a person and about how his life-changing treatment saved her. When she spoke for BIRRDsong, she gushed about having a new life even with a TBI and the feelings of success when she overcame obstacles. In front of these audiences, Joan was passionate and positive, easily connecting her message with her new life.

The change came when she got up in front of the audience at the VIP. Instead of gushing, Joan came across as someone angry and bitter about injustices in the world. Her messages of survival and second chances were intertwined with her frustration about the double standard, leaving her audience confused.

Luckily Susan quickly realized some of the underlying challenges in Joan's presentation. Joan focused on demanding that the audience hear what she had to tell them. If she wanted to be more effective, she needed to flip that around. If Joan could focus on what the audience needed, rather than on what she wanted to tell them, Susan believed she could be effective in a more dramatic way.

Then there was the problem with her overall message. Although Joan had a good story of anger, sorrow and loss, it showcased nothing more than Joan's resentment. Instead, Susan wanted to use Joan's story and her exuberant, effervescent personality to help her speak from the heart about how the decision one person makes can have a dramatic impact on the lives of others.

To do that, Susan knew Joan would have to step away from her vendetta against the military and move toward a message of choice. For Joan, this was going to be a battle. She wasn't about to give up her fight to make the world see the double standard that existed, and she insisted on sharing it with everyone she met.

"I didn't care at that point who was in the audience," Joan said later. "I was there just to deliver the message. I was totally obsessed. I was angry at the government and was going to take it out on them."

Susan didn't want Joan to leave her double-standard message behind. She agreed it was something that needed to be heard. At the same time, she wanted Joan to learn to tailor her presentations to the many audiences she would find as a part of Oregon Impact.

"Oregon Impact is an organization that goes where we are needed and does what is requested," Susan says. As coordinator, she received invitations to a variety of venues, and each venue needed a different aspect of their message. A typical week could include requests for volunteers for the monthly Victim Impact Panel, a high school drunk driving prevention program or a health fair. Anytime there was an opportunity to educate people on the dangers of drinking and driving, Oregon Impact was there.

Susan knew Joan could be a valued speaker for Oregon Impact, if she could bring the same passion there that she showed when she talked about Dr.

Bruce or BIRRDsong. To help her finesse her presentation, Susan tried to help Joan understand she needed to showcase her human side at the VIP in the same way.

"Susan taught me to reach into myself and bring out more of who I am. Instead of just telling a story, Susan taught me how to show the person attached to the story," Joan says.

Susan started by teaching Joan how to break her story into different sections. Some sections were about her past, some about the present and some specifically about the crash. This meant a paradigm shift for Joan. The idea that the audience might only hear a small part of her story didn't make sense to her. How could leaving out the things she considered vital to her story make her a better speaker? How could she have an impact if she didn't tell the whole story?

Joan was still stuck in the idea that she had to *make* people hear her. That meant telling her entire story, every time. Susan struggled to help Joan understand that structuring her presentation to fit the audience could make her more effective.

"Sometimes a targeted 12-minute story is more effective than a 20-minute more elaborate one," Susan told her. Joan wasn't convinced but she was willing to try because she understood Susan was helping her achieve her purpose.

"Other people have tried to help me, and it's like 'Don't tell me what I'm going to say. Don't tell me what I'm going to do,'" Joan says. "Susan would say, 'Let's leave this part out,' and I'd say 'OK' because that's what Susan said. Why? I trusted her. I now had a purpose, which she seemed to be on board with, which in turn showed me that this was the way to follow my purpose and get it accomplished."

"Over time, I think we developed a trust, and Joan felt much more comfortable sharing with me. We would reflect on the audience demographics and what we wanted to leave them with," Susan says. "It's about being successful, not only for you, but for that audience."

To help Joan understand the importance of selecting a different focus of her presentation for each audience, Susan began taking Joan to Oregon Impact presentations around town. By showing her how other speakers successfully focused on what the audience needed, Susan hoped Joan would understand the impact of streamlining her presentation. Joan wanted to believe her, but remained unconvinced.

"Oh sure," she remembers thinking, "those speakers are going to help a few people, but I'm going to change the world."

It took a presentation at a local Rotary Club for Joan to start to see what Susan had been trying to explain. They were there to speak to a group of business owners about the general services offered to businesses by Oregon Impact. It was an entirely different experience than Joan expected. This wasn't a group of people sentenced to attend a VIP. No one in this audience had harmed anyone because of a bad choice. These people were not at all interested in listening to a pompom wielding ex-cheerleader blather on about being a victim of a grand conspiracy. Even worse, when she tried to talk to them about it they ignored her.

Shocked by their apparent indifference to her story, Joan assumed it was a one-time thing. To her surprise, she was sidelined again just weeks later. As part of her ongoing mission, Joan had created a You Tube video called, *There Ought to be a Law*, explaining the military double standard. She then created cards with the website address to pass out to anyone who stood still long enough to take one whenever she went out with Susan.

"I was handing out cards about my YouTube website, and one day Susan said, 'This isn't the place for that. We are talking to people who are offenders, and you are talking about a law. Your message isn't about how to stop a drunk driver. It's about how you were personally impacted by someone who chose to drink and drive.'"

Joan was stunned. Just like at the Rotary meeting, she felt once again that no one cared about her mission. "It's not that no one cares," Susan corrected her. "This is just not the time or place for that part of your message."

Everything that Susan had been trying to tell her finally clicked. After months of explanations, Joan finally understood that if she created different presentations she could reach an even larger number of people.

"It's taking myself out of it and making it about the audience!" Joan says.

Finally understanding the need for multiple presentations opened an entirely new set of opportunities for Joan. Now that Joan was on board, Susan patiently worked to help Joan discover her talents and create presentations that varied from tranquil to robust and rowdy.

"Joan was so passionate, and she got so 'on' that sometimes the passion couldn't be shut off at a time when, maybe in certain audiences, it was too much," Susan says. "At times, exuberance would overfill a room, and that exuberance was not necessary."

Joan struggled with the need to rein in her passion during a presentation. She knew she had enthusiasm, a great presentation and a story to tell. She had a purpose and a mission to share. Wasn't that enough? Sure, she got a little wound up now and then, but shouting and screaming and laughing out loud seemed natural to her. Born to be the center of attention, Joan knew she belonged on stage. So why did it feel like she was doing something wrong? Then one fateful day, Joan learned a hard lesson: It wasn't all about her.

Susan, Joan and three other presenters were invited to speak at a pre-prom program at St. Mary's Academy, Joan's alma mater. Susan designed the presentation so that each volunteer would have 15 minutes on stage and each story would lead directly into the next, building emotion and reinforcing the message of making safe choices. As they waited their turn, Susan reminded the presenters that she would hold up a red card from the back of the room to identify when their time was up. She had done this dozens of times, and it had always gone smoothly. Until today. Today, Joan refused to get off the stage.

"She got on stage, and she was so hyped up," Susan says. "This was one of the places where she shared that fact that she had been a drinker and driver. It worked because of the audience, and it was her school so there was a good strong connection. When it started going too long, I wasn't overly worried, the audience was still engaged."

Joan kept talking, right through the next speaker's allotted time. Susan repeatedly held up the red card only to have Joan ignore her. So she moved from the back of the audience to the front of the stage below, directly in front of Joan, and waved. She still couldn't get Joan's attention.

"I couldn't see her," Joan says. "The lights were in my eyes!"

Susan says, "You were on a high. I stood up and couldn't get her attention, I walked up on the stage, and I was standing there, and she was still ignoring me. I actually finally had to walk up to the podium. It was like I needed a shepherd's hook to pull her off the stage."

When it finally registered that Susan was trying to get her to wrap it up, Joan started giggling. She and Susan made up a spontaneous explanation that left the students laughing, so the presentation ended on a positive note. But Joan's irreverence came with a price. As a result of her refusal to yield the spotlight, one of the other speakers, who had lost her son to an impaired driver, was unable to share her story with the students. Hurt and angry, she blamed both Joan and

Susan for a missed opportunity to share her loss at such an important event.

It was a hard lesson for Joan. "When I have the audience, I want to keep the audience," she says. Excited to be back in her old high school, speaking to teens and doing what she loved, she had completely overlooked the others who were there for the same thing. It broke her heart to realize her selfishness had prevented someone else from having a chance to make a difference. She also felt responsible for the fall-out between Susan and the volunteer, who believed she had been abandoned in favor of Joan.

This was yet another turning point in her life. She saw that being part of Oregon Impact meant being part of a team rather than one person telling her story. What she did, how she behaved, what she said, it all had an impact on others. Sometimes, the impact was on people in the audience. Sometimes, it was on people on the stage with her. Sometimes, it was on the people who ran the organization. No matter how she looked at it, she saw there was more at stake than getting people to listen to her story. Joan knew the time had come for her to change.

"Susan was able to get me to reach in and find Joan, express Joan, to tell people about Joan and to see the mistakes I have made and how they can make better choices than I did. There was such a respect she had for me as a person," Joan says.

"Now, I have more to say and a gentler way to say it. This is the reason Susan is such a big part in my life. She helped me see I was making a difference just by being who I am. I learned that sharing from my heart—and speaking to another person's heart—is when the message is most effective."

Understanding that it was more important to give the audience what they needed to hear, rather than what she wanted to say, helped Joan blossom as a speaker. This made her even more valuable to Susan.

"Because of her story and experiences, we could pick and choose the components of great value that got her the standing ovations or got her the tears. Although I don't know that we got everyone in the audience, and some we got only for a week or two with good decisions, I do believe there are a lot of people who made a commitment to their future right there and then forever."

Oregon Impact volunteers were needed for many different venues, which required Susan to match what the volunteer desired with the available opportunity. Some people wanted to get up on stage to influence safe choices, some wanted to facilitate small groups, and some wanted to man the booth at community events and pass out fliers.

Because of Joan's unpredictability, Susan had been carefully selecting where Joan would speak. Now that she was ready to behave, completely understanding that the message was about the listener rather than the speaker, Susan felt confident Joan was ready to fully join the team of speakers and help get their message out, and she had a special place for her.

One of Susan's challenges came from balancing the volunteer's desire to get information out about impaired driving with respecting people's choice to drink alcohol. The message Oregon Impact provided had to be friendly and caring rather than negative or condemning.

"Drinking is legal, so what does drinking and driving really mean?" Susan asked. "People don't want to talk to you, because they do have a glass of wine or two at a restaurant and then they drive home. They don't want to face their own potential risks. It's hard to engage people in that regard. And if we don't get them in a friendly, open way, there are very few people who will come into the conversation."

Happily, these were the settings where Joan excelled. Unlike some of the volunteers who might have been uncomfortable engaging complete strangers, even on a topic they strongly believed in, Joan was fearless.

"Joan just jumped in. She was not shy. She just has a dynamic about her that works." Susan says.

Joan agrees. "If we were at a fair or something, I would just go out and start talking to someone. Because I loved talking to people it was easy for me. If there was something they said and I could get Oregon Impact in there, I would get it in."

Joan was having a ball. She was out in the community, speaking with more people than she ever could have dreamed and sharing her purpose. Meeting Susan and joining Oregon Impact gave her the opportunity to finally make the difference she had longed for. Even better, in 2008, Joan made her first new friend.

Joan Makes a Friend

When Joan and Susan talk about their first meeting, they both laugh about how expectations don't always meet reality. Joan expected to meet someone who could provide her with opportunities to share her newfound purpose. Susan expected someone who could help expand Oregon Impact's message. What neither expected was a friendship that would completely change Joan's life. When they met for coffee at a local Elmer's Restaurant that first time, they clicked.

"You would have thought we had known each other for 20 years," Susan says.

"It was instant," Joan agrees. "We introduced ourselves and sat down to have coffee and BAM! We didn't stop talking. It was like we were related or had known each other forever. God only knows how much time went by. We could have stayed there for hours."

Discovering a new friend over coffee was a luxury Joan had forgotten existed. In the years since the crash, she had been too busy simply learning to live again to realize she was lonely. Sure, she had John, and she spoke with Shawn at least once a week, but it was no longer enough. Even when surrounded by a family who loved her and many acquaintances, true friends were in short supply.

"In school, making or having lots of friends was just a given," the once popular Joan says. Even in the party days, when true relationships were few and far between, she had lots of drinking buddies. After the crash, things changed. Most of the people who had been friends with Old Joan weren't interested in this new version. On the rare occasion people did want to reconnect, it usually turned out to be more to satisfy a curiosity than to rekindle a friendship.

"I remember meeting up with a woman, a few years after the crash, who was in a business similar to ours, and she said she had heard that I lost half my brain," Joan says unhappily. "Putting up with these misconceptions and the fact that people may have been afraid to stay in contact was disheartening to say the least. I could see people looking at me, people who knew me, watching my gait and talking to me so loudly that I had to tell them that my ears still worked fine."

Even those who wanted to try to build a friendship often found it challenging, if not downright impossible. Extraordinary progress or not, Joan still struggled emotionally. On the outside she looked like an adult, but on the inside she was still a child. Her communication skills were spotty at best. Emotionally unstable, she threw tantrums when overly tired, argued with John when she believed she was right and fought with anyone she felt had wronged her. As a result, most of her relationships were with people in the recovery community. People just like her.

Joan and her fellow survivors often ask each other, "How long have you been out?" rather than, "How old are you?" Instead of defining age by the date they were born, these survivors started the clock at the point they left rehab. It was both a congratulatory statement and a way to understand where the person was in their recovery process. Someone who had been *out* one or two years faced a completely different set of obstacles than someone who had been *out* seven or eight. This gave a frame of reference for what to expect when speaking with each other, an important consideration that people who were not familiar with the rehab community didn't always understand.

In 2008, Joan had been *out* for almost nine years and was considered an exceptional example of what a survivor could accomplish. At the same time, in some ways she was still a child desperately seeking someone to play with. Like any other child, Joan wanted to find someone who would accept her for who she was, as she was, with all her flaws and faults. Sadly, finding that friend seemed futile. It didn't seem anyone in the outside world wanted to play with her. Then she met Susan.

Susan was the first person to come into Joan's life who wasn't family, from the rehab community or from her past. Susan saw her as a real, vital person instead of someone damaged. She had never known the Old Joan, didn't know Rehab Joan and had no preconceptions about the person standing in front of her. After all these years, an overjoyed Joan had finally made a new friend.

"Susan was the first person who was out of the rehab box," Joan says. "She was someone I could completely pour my heart out to. She was the person I could play jacks with, and if I stole a jack she wouldn't get mad."

Susan explains that she didn't see herself as anyone special for accepting Joan as she was. She believes their friendship grew, as most do, simply from the time they spent together.

"Because she didn't work, Joan was always available and lived close, so I could pick her up and take her to the various events," she says. During those endless car rides from presentation to presentation, they got to know one another.

The conversations started as most of Joan's stories did, with her amazing recovery, her sense of purpose, her drive to change the world, but Susan came to believe that she wasn't getting the whole story behind her new friend's incredible life. As time went on, she put bits and pieces of their conversations together and began to figure out Joan was hiding something involving her past that she obviously didn't want to discuss.

"I sensed shame from that whole part of her life," Susan says, but she didn't consider it anything that could derail their friendship. In Susan's mind everyone had a past filled with mistakes and missteps. If Joan wanted to talk about it, she was there to listen. If not, that was fine, too. She put Joan's reluctance to go into detail down to a sense of embarrassment about who she had been before the crash and let it go. For Susan, it was a non-issue.

It wasn't that easy for Joan. Excited as she was to make a new friend, Joan worried about what Susan would think about her if she learned about who she had been. Part of her fear came from the struggle she was having herself in reconciling the actions of Old Joan with the life of New Joan.

Making Peace with Old Joan

Joan understood the kind of person she had been, and it made her uncomfortable to think others still saw her that way. She understood only too well the accusations of hypocrisy that could come if people heard her entire life story. Here she was telling offenders about life as a victim, all the while knowing it easily could have been Old Joan out there in the audience.

She feared that many would call it Karma, thinking she had gotten what she deserved and that her actions in the past somehow detracted from her actions in the present. She was afraid she would be blamed for her actions in a life she barely remembered living and that people would no longer value what she had to offer. The conflict left her confused and worried, so she tried to ignore it.

"I didn't want to talk about it because if I didn't talk about it didn't exist," she says.

Pushing aside her fears, Joan finally gathered up the courage to tell Susan the truth about Old Joan. To her shock, Susan cared less about what she had done wrong in the past and more how she could use her poor choices to make a difference. Instead of abandoning her, Susan showed Joan how she could apply her past to become more powerful in the present.

"It was not just about the drinking and the behaviors that went along with that, but what it meant to her young life," Susan says about Joan's reluctance to share those stories. "I think there was a desire to not really frame anything around that part of the message. There was avoidance. And then when she became a victim, it made it even worse because she realized what she could have done."

With Susan's help, Joan finally began to understand how to reconcile her past mistakes. Susan encouraged her to use her past instead of fearing it, teaching her to focus on what she could learn from those experiences. This idea of looking forward intrigued her, but Joan still couldn't let the past go completely. She couldn't wrap her mind around the idea that everyone makes mistakes when they are young. She couldn't forgive herself for some of the things Old Joan had done.

Then came the amazing day when everything changed. As they were driving to an event, Joan shared that she had been pregnant as a teenager and had given her baby up for adoption. Embarrassed by the actions of her teenage self, Joan hung her head and waited for Susan's condemnation.

"I looked at her and said, 'But you were 17,'" Susan says. "It hurt her so much in her heart, and I'm looking at it saying, 'But you were 17.'"

Susan understood that beneath Joan's adult exterior there was a scared little girl, and she wasn't going to hold Joan responsible in the present for the choices she had made in the past. This was yet another shift in Joan's understanding of relationships. She had just confided something that she was sure would make Susan think less of her and Susan's response was baffling. For the first time Joan understood that everyone made mistakes. It wasn't because of the brain injury. It was because she was growing up. Susan helped Joan realized that she could make a bad choice without the world ending. She could make a mistake, as long as she learned from it.

In this, Susan explained to Joan, she was like every other teenager on the planet. Bad choices didn't mean she was a bad person. They meant she was human. It was time for Joan to decide what she was going to do next. She could either ignore her mistakes or learn from the lesson that came with them. Either way, Susan would be there to listen, no matter what Joan wanted to share.

Susan showed Joan that her friends wouldn't abandon her for doing something that might be seen as stupid or careless.

"I had never had a friend I could share my gut-wrenching ugliness with and still feel safe," Joan says. "I've shared things with her that I have never shared with anyone else, even Shawn or Husband, and she allowed it. She made it OK to look inside myself and be OK with the bad decisions I'd made."

This understanding and support allowed Joan to grow in leaps and bounds. She began to try new things rather than stick to a set routine. She explored beyond the boundaries she had set for herself. She stopped beating herself up when something went wrong and started looking for the lesson instead. With Susan's help, Joan began to focus on enjoying the journey, discovering new avenues and experiences, even if that meant tripping and falling the entire way.

"The impact you have had on my life has been so unbelievably important," Joan tells Susan. "Instead of people enabling me by saving me from doing things wrong, Susan would let me make a mistake and then encourage me to do it another way."

Receiving this encouragement to make mistakes and learn from them was yet another new experience for Joan. Susan was the first person who didn't worry, deep in her heart that Joan would die if something went wrong. Instead, she offered a type of freedom Joan had never known.

Joan knew her family loved her, and they never tried to hold her back from experimenting. John, Shawn, and all of the extended family encouraged her to get out and about. They wanted her to have independence, to be brave and to experience all life had to offer. Joan also understood they lived with constant underlying fears they couldn't escape each time she walked out the door. They had seen her almost die. They had seen her fight for years to come back. They had seen her make bad choices and be hurt, emotionally and physically. For them, the stakes were incredibly high. A Joan who took risks and made mistakes was a Joan they needed to worry about.

Susan, on the other hand, had never seen that Joan. She didn't worry.

"I think there was a new turn in her life after meeting Susan," John says. "Susan was just the first friend that wasn't from the past. Susan was very strong, accomplished, intelligent and loyal. She was a good friend and had the effect of transferring some of those traits over to Joan. They sort of brushed off.

Because of Susan's influence, Joan became more confident."

Much of that confidence came simply from how Susan viewed Joan. She wasn't particularly interested in who Joan used to be. Susan liked Joan for who she was now. When Susan looked at Joan she saw someone funny, engaging and real. Sure, Joan might wobble a bit when she walked and forget things now and then, but it was no big deal. She was still a hoot to be around. After nine years, Joan had finally found a new friend.

As their friendship grew, so did Susan's importance to Joan's mission to change the world. Susan had a unique ability to reflect Joan's words and help her see them from a different angle.

"She taught me to look inside me, to stop blaming and start living. She taught me to start sharing what had happened to help instead of doing the blame game," Joan says. "She did it just by being who she was, by edifying my inner strengths. I've always been one to say, 'Tell me what I can do' and not focus on what I've lost, but I was stuck in blaming mode. She got me out of that."

"As a result of those choices and what happened to me, I could then make an impact on other people and prevent them from making bad choices. I had never seen it that way. I don't know that Susan necessarily said it in words; however, with the friendship and the trust that I have for her, I was okay with, 'This is what I need to do.'"

"Her guidance allowed me to look into myself and bring what was inside of me out, so I could reach more people. She would validate everything I was going to be doing. She would say, 'This makes a difference to these people, so do that.'"

Joan's life was racing forward, and now she had someone to play with along the way. Things were once again looking up.

Learning to Listen

Joan's belief in herself grew rapidly as the months went on. This gift of friendship was one she didn't realize she had been missing, but now that she knew what it was like, she wanted others to feel it also. She wanted to be a "Susan," bringing friendship and acceptance to another's troubled life. She wanted to be someone else's "Shawn," showing how love can help heal. She wanted to help others learn about their brand new life. She wanted to help others in the same way so many others had helped her. Interestingly, she didn't realize she was already filling that need for many people in her life.

Joan knew when she walked up to the podium at the VIP, the people in the audience were there only because attending the panel was part of their court-mandated requirements. It didn't mean they would pay attention. As she poured her heart out, month after month, she could only hope they learned from what she had to say.

To Joan's constant surprise, they did. At the end of every presentation, attendees surrounded her. They wanted her opinions. They wanted her suggestions. They wanted her knowledge. Joan slowly began to see her value.

She saw it when one of Dr. Bruce's students said he was going to pursue studies in vision therapy after hearing her speak. She saw it after the VIP when a drunk driver cried and said he was sorry. It was there at BIRRDsong meetings when she shared her experiences with people who didn't know what to do next, and the families cried with relief that they had found the resources they so desperately needed. It was even there at RIO, when she wandered from room to room offering help and hope. Joan was no longer just a speaker. Without even realizing it, she had become a mentor. It was a surprising revelation.

Joan knew she was sharing her purpose by telling her stories, but she never saw herself as someone making a difference in a one-on-one setting. Even during the creation of BIRRDsong, she thought of herself as part of a team, developing resources and information to ease the path of survivors as they navigated this strange new world.

It was through her work with the people at RIO and BIRRDsong that Joan finally realized all she had to offer. She could mentor people through their entire recovery process. She could work with others, using all the things she had learned to change individual lives. At the same time, despite everything she had accomplished, Joan understood her limitations. She wasn't a trained counselor, doctor or therapist. She was willing to share what she knew in the hopes that it could help, but she was muddling along, hoping she was doing it correctly.

As Joan began to question her abilities, she received a call from a MADD coordinator asking if she would be willing to attend a four-day Victim Advocate Training Program in Dallas. There, she would learn to guide victims through the bewildering world of the justice system, provide information and referrals specifically designed for those affected by drunk drivers and learn how to offer overall emotional support correctly. Joan was ecstatic. This was exactly the kind of training she needed. She couldn't wait to go.

There was only one problem. Texas was a long way from Joan's hometown of Portland, Ore. John wanted to be supportive, but he couldn't get the time off work, and he had no intention of letting her travel that far on her own. So, he called Shawn. "I said absolutely, I would be interested," Shawn says. Taking days off work, flying to Texas and signing up to be a Victim Advocate was simply a way to acknowledge all that Joan had accomplished. Although Shawn didn't necessarily see herself as a mentor or advocate, the opportunity to be a part of something so important to Joan thrilled her.

As she boarded the plane an excited Joan couldn't stop thinking about all she was going to learn. She would return to Portland as an official, certified advocate, with all the knowledge she would need to be a mentor.

In Dallas, Joan was amazed to find hundreds of people just like her. These were people who could relate to what she and her family had gone through over the past few years. They understood the suffering and pain that could come from someone else's poor choice, and yet they refused to be defined as victims. They were resilient. They were survivors. Like her, these people had come to Dallas to learn how to do something good with what had happened to them. They wanted to learn to help others. And unlike most of the people Joan met on a day-to-day basis, there was no "poor little Joan" mentality in this group.

"It was such a good experience, because there were so many people there who had gone through this kind of experience with a drunk-driving related injury or death. All the empathy was amazing. Joan wasn't any kind of victim in their eyes, because she wasn't a victim in her eyes," Shawn says.

Although excited by everything the conference offered, Joan found learning some skills much tougher than she expected. Learning to be still and listen, for example, was particularly challenging. The instructor explained that a successful mentor or advocate has to listen without interrupting or interjecting. She has to be patient, allowing as much time as necessary to really hear what is being said. Even with all her practice over the past few years, Joan had still not perfected this particular technique. In fact, when she honestly evaluated her listening skills, she had to admit she had been doing the exact opposite. Even with Susan's help, Joan's focus often slipped into telling people what she believed they needed to hear. Changing that approach around would require a fundamental shift in her thought process. For the effervescent and stubborn Joan, it would be a tremendous challenge.

Shawn remembers one exercise designed to specifically test Joan's ability to remain quiet and listen. In this challenge, Joan had to sit across from Shawn, look into her eyes and not speak. As time went on, Joan began to wiggle and bounce in her chair.

"It was making me a mess!" she says.

Finally, the facilitator called the time and allowed everyone to speak. A frustrated Joan insisted the silence had gone on for at least an hour. In reality, it had been a whopping 10 seconds.

When the instructor asked Joan why she had such a hard time staying still and not speaking, she replied, "Because I just love her so much."

"That got a collective 'aaawwww' from the room," Shawn says.

It had been years since Joan had the chance to learn something entirely new and different and this new opportunity was thrilling. In exercises after exercise, she learned specific skills to provide emotional support to others and to help fellow survivors navigate the world of a victim without feeling like one.

"I was able, through that training process, to learn how to listen, how to talk, what to say, what not to say and trigger points that might escalate a situation."

It might have been tough, but it was an exciting, intensive adventure that Joan cherished, even though she was completely worn out by early afternoon each day.

"By 1:30 every day Joan was toast," Shawn says.

When Joan returned home at the end of the training program, she was ready to race out to help others, especially those at RIO and BIRRDsong. She had a whole new basket of tips and resources from MADD. She had all the tricks Michelle had used back in those dark days at RIO. She remembered Teresia's mantra, "You don't get your old life back; you get a brand new life." She was ready to be the perfect mentor.

Adventures in Mentoring

By 2011 Joan had the presentations, props, knowledge and confidence she needed to talk with victims, offenders, and students about drunk driving in any venue she found. But her true gift was for working with those who had brain injuries. They trusted her because she was one of them. She knew what they were feeling. She knew every excuse they were going to come up with, because she had already tried them herself, and she wasn't going to take any complaining from the whiners. Either they wanted her help, or she would move on to those who did. The hospital staff might be required to deal with those who didn't want to succeed, but Joan didn't have time for crybabies.

"If someone is willing to crawl through the tunnel of rehab and see there's a light on the other end, it'll be me holding a flashlight, extending my hand to help guide and pull them through," Joan says. She is there, willing to help them fight for their new lives, but only if they are willing.

"You cannot use a brain injury for any type of excuse," Joan says. "I remember when I first came home from the hospital, and I did something stupid, and I said, 'Oh, I have a brain injury.' My sister Lisa looked at me and said, 'I'll give you two weeks with that, and then that's the last I'm going to hear that.' And I thought, 'Holy crap! I'm gonna be held accountable completely."

Annoying as it was at the time, Joan soon came to understand that having people hold her accountable was much of why she eventually improved. In return, she planned to pass this lesson on to those she worked with, regardless of how upsetting they found it.

Joan knows some people can become so overwhelmed by the sheer magnitude of their injuries that they shut down. Does she understand how they feel? Yes. Is she willing to allow them to use it as an excuse? Absolutely not.

"Once they learn respect for their injury and don't let it hold them hostage or use it as an excuse, they have nowhere to move but forward," she says. "I tell them, 'Your life now is a blank canvas, and you are the artist. You not only get to choose the colors you want to use, you have control of where the paint goes and how the picture turns out. Where you may not have had control in your life before, you are now the one who has the control and can determine how fast or slow you go.'"

Joan loved helping but struggled when those she mentored didn't respond as quickly as she wanted. She often forgot that she was years ahead of these patients and that she had to give them the time they needed to catch up. When she found herself frustrated with someone who was not progressing, she reminded herself of the toast and puzzle exercises from her days in RIO. Remembering those horrible, confusing days helped her be more patient with where these people were and how she could best help them. Along the way she learned that helping sometimes meant being less aggressive, not more. Sometimes, pushing, demanding or even encouraging didn't work. Sometimes, helping meant simplifying.

"People in general have a tendency to overcomplicate the simplest thing, and with brain injury, your new world is already complex," she says. "What I try to do as a mentor is teach those with brain injuries how to use what is already in their world and make adjustments for the way it fits into their world now. If they don't have a drastic change to make, don't. Just keep working with whatever they have until it works for them. And when it doesn't seem to be working, put it down and move on. It's gotta be easy enough to understand and remember."

When asked how she had succeeded, Joan demonstrates what she had learned, the different behaviors that worked for her, and offers suggestions the professionals might not have considered. It was a delicate dance. She didn't want to interfere with the therapy process or step on the toes of the doctors. She had great respect for these hardworking people who knew how to heal physical injuries. After all, they were the people who had helped her. At the same time, Joan could see things from the other side. She could approach problems from a practical perspective, offering a view that might be completely different from the one found in a textbook: views on the concept of time, for example.

"I'm unable to grasp time. If I'm not wearing a watch or near a clock, I have no idea how long I've been doing something—or what time of the day it is for that matter. I can't even begin to figure out space in time, either. What I mean by this is, how long the morning lasts as it goes into afternoon and afternoon into evening."

"Today, when I was at the gym, I looked at a clock on the wall, and apparently, it had stopped at 7:20 a.m. I was totally dumbfounded. I knew I had gotten there at 9:00 a.m., and I couldn't figure out for the life of me how I went back in time. Seriously, it really stumped me."

"Weeks, years, it's all foreign to me. Everything was a week ago, a year ago or yesterday. I'm unable to retain time relating to how long something lasted, how long something takes to complete, things of that nature. I can get where I have to go, but have no idea after I'm there how long it took to get there."

This was the sympathetic ear Joan offered to those who no longer understood how hours turned into days and days into weeks. Personally, she knew how the loss of the ability as simple as telling time would have a profound impact on day-to-day activities.

The doctors, physical therapists and counselors offered practical exercises to improve brain function. Joan, on the other hand, could offer the tricks she had learned to overcome problems and how to keep a sense of humor when she couldn't.

"Take what happened in the process of your rehab, grab the happy thoughts, and move forward with it," she would tell her fellow brain injury survivors. "It's about shifting your focus."

Joan admits she is tough on those who come to her for help. Her goal is to help them move forward, and she doesn't allow any non-productive whining. She acknowledges that in some circumstances, people with a brain injury are not physically able to progress due to their injury, and she sympathizes with them. At the same time, she remains vocal about those who choose to use their injury as a reason not to try.

"Can't is not a word I can identify with," she says. If she could do it, they can at least try. She turns compliments about her success into challenges for her mentees.

"One woman I mentored made references on many occasions to my great attitude and said she wished she could have a better attitude. I told her that's something she can control," Joan says.

Anger is another emotion Joan refuses to encourage in those who want her help. She agrees that although anger is sometimes a natural or necessary emotion, survivors need to see it as something they need to control rather than being controlled by it.

When they objected she told them, "If you get angry I understand, but it will zap your energy. I get angry. I get pissed, but it has to be for a short time."

Joan helps those she mentors redirect their emotions, getting their focus away from the anger and into something more positive. "You have to get them away from the thought that they are going to get angry, because that is something they will hold on to. Once they are angry, they can't get past it."

As word of Joan and her no-nonsense approach spread throughout the brain injury community, professionals began to take notice that she could sometimes get through to the patients when no one else could.

Joan beams as she remembers, "One of the coolest things to ever happen to me was when I walked in the door for an appointment with Dr. Bruce and he said, 'Oh thank God you're here! Will you please go talk with one of my patients who is so angry?'"

"His name was Jeff. He was angry and confused and thought he was all alone. When I first met him, the biggest challenge was his anger—anger at how he got injured and the fact that people, of course, didn't understand. On our initial meeting, I identified the fact that he was angry and that he had every right to be. However, I also told him that if he got lost in the anger and let it consume him, he would never move on and find the 'New Jeff.' I told him the old Jeff was gone, and the sooner he recognized the 'New Jeff'' the sooner he'd have success."

It was a brutal first meeting, but Joan never wavered. As a fellow survivor she had the right to call him out for his behavior, and it led to a friendship that Joan has treasured for years.

"I think what I mostly did for him was validate his feelings and help him understand it was OK to tell people if he was unable to do something. He had nothing to be ashamed of, and in fact, he had a lot of fun when he learned to laugh some of the stuff off. I told him, 'Bury that person. Take what you have and expand from there. Find something you can do now and enjoy.' And he did. Over the last few years, his growth has been stupendous," Joan says.

Joan's unique abilities as a mentor also apply to helping the injured understand how those without injuries view them. Often, according to Joan, survivors get stuck in an "I have a brain injury" loop, expecting each random passerby to see that there is something wrong and react accordingly. They want the world to notice and adapt to their disabilities. They expect constant praise from family and friends on how well they have worked to fix their problems. Because they see themselves as broken, they expect others to see them that same way.

Not surprisingly, Joan takes issue with this mentality. She wants people to see themselves as functioning members of society, not as damaged goods. They are survivors, not victims.

Joan's goal is to do whatever is necessary to help those around her. She wants them to learn to honor their injury, but not let it define them. She wants to help them get better. Much to her surprise, she finds herself falling back on the techniques her 'nemesis,' Michelle, had used back in those long-ago days in RIO. As frustrating and demeaning as they may have felt, Joan can't argue with success.

"My friend with a brain injury struggled with word finding. I knew the word she wanted, but I had to wait and let her say it. I had to let her work it out. Unless a person says, 'I can't find it, would you help?' I don't help. Even when they ask for help, I only do it a little. For example, I would say to her, 'I know the word you're looking for, and it starts with a 'P'."

Joan burst out laughing when she realized she has become the hated "Michelle" to her mentees and friends, but she doesn't care. She knows what tricks work and that she is a better mentor when she uses them. She wants to help survivors learn to overcome their frustration without enabling them. She wants to help them learn to make toast, even when they can't find the toaster.

"It may make you angry, because it did with me. But you will move through the anger and you will learn," Joan reassures those she mentors. "It is part of the journey to your new life."

Since she thoroughly enjoys mentoring, Joan was astonished to find that there was a dark side to the process. To her amazement, not everyone was willing to do the work, regardless of how much help they had. Some people simply find the journey too difficult to continue once they started, while others flat-out refuse to begin. At first Joan took these devastating failures personally. Trying to help those who didn't want her help was exhausting, futile and frustrating, and often ended with her neglecting those who did want her guidance. Joan's wakeup call finally came when she found herself sucked into a relationship based on enabling rather than mentoring.

"I thought we had a close friendship and I felt really good all-around, but what I really ended up doing was enabling her," Joan says. "She was an alcoholic with a brain injury who had been having a really rough time, and I wanted to help. Then I found out she was still drinking and driving, with me in her car! Her decision to choose alcohol was hard because I had put so much energy into her. I even had my family involved in helping her. I had so many people vested in this one woman. It was a big slap in the face and a huge lesson for me to learn. I had to learn to not give myself away. I had to learn not to enable."

Learning not to enable included overcoming the hurt feelings that came from finding out that someone she considered a friend was just using her. She had to accept that not everyone wanted her help, no matter how much she wanted them to get better. Joan had to learn she couldn't save everyone.

This incident also taught Joan that not everyone in her life cared about keeping her safe. The realization that someone she was trying to help would drive drunk with her in the car, intentionally putting her in danger, was almost more than she could comprehend. She felt taken advantage of and betrayed.

"It's part of who Joan is," John says. "She's just very unselfish, and she tends to trust too much."

"It's a constant journey," Joan says. "Because of the lessons I learned from that experience, I can now see me doing too much. If I want to do something for someone, I consciously step back and suggest they do it themselves. I say, 'Why don't you try that yourself, and let me know how that goes.'"

As a brain injury survivor, Joan was at great risk of people taking advantage of her, especially in the mentor role or when speaking at a VIP. When it came to helping, Joan was like an exuberant Labrador puppy. She loved everyone and wanted to play. Joan took people at face value. If someone said they would be her friend, she believed them. If they said they needed her help, she helped. It never dawned on her there were people in the world who might try to harm her or have less-than-honorable intentions. Much to John's despair, Joan had not regained an awareness of dishonesty or disreputable behavior.

"There were several times after a presentation when she would give her phone number out or volunteer to help someone without knowing a thing about them," he says. "After the fact, I had to step in and ask, 'Do you think that's a good idea?' or 'What were you thinking?'"

Once again John had to become a master manipulator to help Joan learn to be more careful. This time, he did it by planting the idea that if she was more selective about which person she chose to help, she could be more effective. If she believed that by avoiding helping someone who seemed sketchy, she would benefit someone else, she would do it.

Much to John's relief, Joan had also developed a circle of people she could trust with instincts that were more advanced than hers. If they told her that someone's motives might be questionable, she would stop and try to understand what they meant. She may not have believed it, but she was willing to take their opinions to heart as a way to protect herself. This reliance on others allowed her to keep her puppy energy and enthusiasm while still staying safe.

If all else failed, she reminded herself about the bar she had set all those years ago when she first became a volunteer.

"What would Husband think about what I'm about to do?" she would ask herself. "Would this make him uncomfortable? Are there consequences to what I'm doing that will upset him?" If the answer to any of those questions was "yes," she would stop and regroup.

With the help of her husband, and her willingness to listen to those around her, Joan's ability to work in the world as a mentor, advocate and speaker increased by leaps and bounds.

A Lesson in Law: Part Two

Joan's life was flying along, and it seemed she had it all. She was a sought-after mentor and advocate. She had the perfect story for the VIP. She understood her purpose and knew she could make a difference. BIRRDsong was continuing as the one-stop shopping organization she had envisioned as a place to support those with brain injuries and their families.

She should have been happy with all of her successes, but her inability to hold the government accountable for allowing drunk personnel to leave their bases without a thought for those who may be in their path continued to frustrate her. She had contacted senators, the media and representatives of the military, anyone she could think of. It didn't help. No one seemed to care. It was always the same response, "Oh how sad, now let it go and move on."

Letting go wasn't an option. John and Joan wanted to believe that someday they would get the justice they deserved, and they were not going to quit until everyone knew about this appalling double standard. Or at least that's what they believed until 2012, when a random meeting with her attorney, John Etter, led Joan to a truth that rocked her to the core.

After years of believing she was a victim of a grand conspiracy to protect the military, Joan learned she had misunderstood what she had been told in 2006. The U.S. government wasn't hiding behind legalese as a way to refuse to cover her medical bills. They weren't "Sending out loaded weapons" and putting U.S.

citizens at risk. There was no hidden agenda protecting bars on bases. In fact, there were strict nationwide laws in place that applied specifically to service members who drank and drove.

Those laws just didn't apply in Joan's situation.

The truth, Etter explained, was hidden in how Utah's Dram Shop law was written. Their entire case had hinged on the wording of the Utah law and the definitions of the words *negligence, right of recovery* and *strict liability.*

Negligence, Etter explained, meant a person has committed a wrongful act by failing to perform to an accepted standard, and it resulted in an injury. If the Utah law included *negligence* and *right of recovery*, Joan and John could have been financially compensated for at least part of the costs they incurred during Joan's long recovery and future costs. But Utah didn't use either of those words in their statute. Instead, the Utah Dram Shop law used the words *strict liability.*

Strict liability meant a person engaged in risky activity that caused harm. In a bar setting, it could have applied to both the patron and the person who served him because both are engaging in an activity that has potential risks—such as drunk driving.

From the outside, it looked like the two laws meant the same thing. The Utah dram shop law should have covered Joan and John, because they could prove liability on the part of the bar for over-service. There was only one problem. The driver was drinking at a bar on federal land, and the federal government could be sued only for negligence. Similar as the laws were, it all came down to semantics.

It was almost inconceivable to Joan. Were these words really the only thing that had prevented them from winning their case? How could this be? What happened to the conspiracy?

Joan listened, stunned, to Etter review what had really happened during the lawsuit. She hadn't been wronged by a shadowy conspiracy. The military wasn't out to protect itself. There was no hidden agenda. Instead, three little words in a state law blocked her right to recover damages from the military bar, simply because of its location. Everything she knew suddenly crumbled to the ground.

As hard as it was for her to wrap her mind around, she was just a victim of a poorly worded law. Even worse: 10 years later, nothing had changed. Although all it would have required was for the Utah legislature to change the state statute to allow the "right to recovery for negligence" in the dram shop law, the law remained the same. It made Joan livid. After all, there were still military bases in Utah, people still drank alcohol, and some still made bad choices. Even if changing the wording of the law wouldn't help her, Joan wanted to protect future victims.

"If something had been done years ago, after the first time this happened, how many lives could have been saved?" she asked. "There are people who live right down the street from Hill Air Force Base, in Ogden, Utah, who have no idea they have no recourse if they are hit by a drunk leaving the base."

The meeting with John Etter upended Joan's world. As she walked out of his office that fateful day with her new understanding of the law, she had to accept that much of what she had believed and fought for over the previous 10 years was wrong. There was no *Joan against the U.S. government*. She had dedicated her life to righting a greater wrong, to protecting the world against a faceless government organization that blatantly flouted laws everyone else had to live by, only to find out that it didn't exist.

It was a harsh reality for Joan to face. She was no different from the dozens of other people who stood at the VIP telling their stories in the hopes that it would make someone change their behavior. She was just another victim of one person's bad choice. She wasn't anyone special after all.

Forgiveness Doesn't Mean Forgetting

Joan honestly believed she had long ago forgiven the drunk driver for what he had done. Even during her time in RIO, when she could barely speak, she wanted people to know she had forgiven him and was moving on with her life. Joan might have been angry over her situation, but she directed her anger at the government that refused to take responsibility for what had happened to her. She wanted to believe it was those responsible for the employees of the bar on the Air Force Base who created this event. They were the ones who allowed the poor airman to walk out the door that fateful night and drive away drunk, forever changing both her life and his. She had forgiven the driver, but she had no intention of forgiving the government. Or so she thought.

"Because I was so fixated on bringing awareness to the wrongdoing of the government, I allowed everyone else to skate," she says. "The driver was guilty because he was drinking; the servers were even guiltier for continuing to serve him."

This realization, accepting that she was just another victim, resonated in Joan's soul. Because one man drank, because the waitress or the bartender, or the other customers didn't choose to try to stop him, life as she knew it ended. It was that simple. And Joan didn't know what to think.

She suddenly saw herself in a whole new way. She wasn't a martyr struggling against the wrongs of the mighty. She wasn't on a mission to save the world, to rewrite laws, to hold the government accountable. She was just another of the thousands of people whose lives had been undone by the poor choices of another. And she was furious, not only at the cost to her life, but also to John's.

"I have an extreme anger, almost a hatred, for what he did to Husband and for what Husband had to go through," she finally says. "Especially right after the crash. To have to hear that his wife may not live, and if she does, the damage could be extensive enough that she may be a vegetable, is too much to forgive. The thought of Husband sleeping on the couch for a month because the bed was too big without me in it while I was up in RIO angers me to the core."

It wasn't surprising that she is angry. Even today, it is still a day-to-day battle to live a somewhat normal life. Every time she looks in the mirror, or trips over a curb, or gets a migraine, she remembers she is paying the price for someone who just had to drink that last beer.

"I guess every time I drop something, because my hands and head aren't working together, or my eyes are really giving me trouble, or just when I'm not able to do things I'm pretty sure I was able to do before my injury, I feel anger toward him," she says. "This takes in everything I'm challenged with, from fatigue to the inability to work or drive."

Trips out into public are a constant reminder of her differences. The sheer information overload during a simple visit to the grocery store is often just too much for her to process. "Visually, a store is overwhelming. Looking at the shelves with all the stuff is crazy. I absolutely hate trying to find something in the area with the aspirin and stuff. Holy shit! Why are there so many choices for a certain product?" she says.

Even 16 years after the crash Joan still can't shop alone because she is incapable of pushing a cart without running it into people or stands. "Then you have the people in the store who aren't watching their kids, and the kids are running all over. Crap!" she says. "I can hear the buggers coming, but can't turn my head fast enough to see them, and if they're not watching for me, which of course they're not, I can't see them, and when I do, it's normally too late. So I try and get out of the way and pray there's something around I can stabilize myself on before they knock me over."

A trip to the mall became an exercise in futility. Not only is there too much to look at, too many people and too much sound, but there is the added challenge of getting to the second or third floor. For most people, an escalator represents just a set of moving stairs. For Joan, it is an optical illusion of never-ending lines. To get on the step, she would have to stand at the base of the escalator, wait until her brain figured out the floor is moving, take a careful step forward, then wait to gain her balance.

"If I don't do this, I'll completely lose track about where I am in space and time. It's frightening! And if someone is trying to talk to me during this, I'm a goner!" she says.

"If Husband's with me, he sets up an invisible safety perimeter so no one can get too close, and I have plenty of space. If I'm on a crowded elevator, you can most certainly count on me holding hands with the person I'm riding with, and if I'm alone, I'll wait until everyone is off, then venture out."

Going to the mall without John or Shawn at her side often leaves Joan at the mercy of friends who don't always understand how difficult it is for her to navigate in her world.

"For me to be able to go out, they would have to slow down, focus on what they were doing and saying, and accommodate my needs in order for me to be safe," Joan says. Not everyone got it.

"I went to lunch with a friend at Clackamas Town Center, and we were going to do a little shopping. During lunch I mentioned that, if by chance, I lose her, I won't be looking for her. I will remain where I am, and she'll need to come get me. I explained that if I get lost it's not only scary, it's dangerous. She seemed to understand. HAH!"

"After lunch, we started walking the mall and doing a little window shopping. When there's someone I'm with that requires me to focus, that's my objective: to stay focused. But she didn't understand. She saw something, darted into the store while talking a mile a minute, and needless to say, I lost her."

"I stayed where I was, just like I said I'd do, and when she finally found me she said, 'What happened to you? You were right behind me.' I was so frustrated. I was never right behind her. The problem was she was talking so she hadn't noticed that we got separated."

This need to rely on others when she is out and about wears on Joan, but even worse are the days when the pain that is her constant companion keeps her from even leaving the house. Sometimes, it is just a dull overall ache, sometimes it is overwhelming fatigue and sometimes it is sudden, intense pain that leaves her unable to function without help.

"For example, one day I was at the grocery store looking at the produce, and all of a sudden it felt like somebody was drilling into the top of my head. There was no sound, just an extreme, acute, direct, very sharp, debilitating pain. The pain was so intense it almost brought me to my knees, and I had to reach out to Husband, so I wouldn't fall to the ground. It only lasted about a minute, but once it was over, my balance was off, and I had to grab my sunglasses because my sensitivity to light kicked in, and I felt blinded."

"We had to leave the grocery store immediately, so Husband could get me home, because after one of these episodes I have to get somewhere quiet and dark to rest. If I don't, I get a migraine that can stay for hours."

To make matters worse, each time Joan goes into public she knows people notice her disabilities and that frustrates her. She doesn't want others to feel sorry for her, but whether she likes it or not, people can't help feel sympathy for her. When she sees people staring at her or pitying her, the anger that bubbles right under the surface can explode. On a bad day, something as innocuous as a compliment by a random stranger can trigger her anger.

"I was at the Department of Motor Vehicles one day getting my ID card, and I smiled at an elderly gentleman when he made a comment about my cute haircut and how much women pay for their hairstyles," she says. "This was when my hair was growing back after my cranioplasty and was very short. Not peach fuzz but short."

"He then saw the scar on the side of my head and his head dropped. The look on his face was both embarrassment and sorrow. The fact that this sweet old man had to feel that anguish, all because of a very selfish and sick drunk driver made me furious!"

These constant reminders of how people view her created a struggle in her mind. She wanted to say she had forgiven the driver for what he had done. It made her feel like a better person, one who could forget and move on. If she could do that, she could stand in front of the VIP audience every month and honestly tell them she believed they were victims of circumstances who deserved a second chance.

The only thing stopping her was her refusal to accept how angry she was. Like a pebble thrown into a pond, the ripples went everywhere. When she looked at total strangers, she saw people who viewed her as someone damaged looking back. When she looked at her friends and family, she saw how they struggled to come to terms with what had happened and how she had changed. When she looked at John, she saw how hurt he was about the changes in both of their lives. Joan could stomp her feet and scream that she was over it all she wanted, but the reality was that she was angry.

The only thing that had made it bearable was her vendetta against the government. As long as she could blame "them," she could get some distance between her anger and her reality. Now, Joan had to accept how furious she was that this entire situation came from the result of just one man's poor decision making.

To move forward and get her life back on track, she had to let go of that anger, to find a way to channel it into something that would allow her to continue her plan to make the world a better place. She needed to incorporate all she had learned, all she felt, all her anger into her purpose.

Joan believed in the VIP mission that encouraged her to treat the drunk drivers she spoke to as people who had made a bad decision rather than bad people. If she were honest with herself, however, her main goal for getting up to the podium had been to educate anyone who would listen about the double standard. Focusing her attention there made it easier for her to live with her situation. She didn't have an emotional connection with the audience members, because she didn't hold them accountable for their actions. They were victims, just like her.

After meeting with Etter and learning the truth about her misunderstood beliefs, she began to second-guess herself. If she wasn't speaking out about the double standard, what story did she have to tell? Was she a hypocrite if she stood in front of the VIP audience and spoke about second chances, when she had not forgiven the person who injured her? Could she forgive and move on?

Living the Purpose

Forgiveness was going to be more challenging than Joan wanted to admit. For years she had tried to focus on the good things she could bring to someone else's life despite what had happened to her. For the brain injured, she was a mentor, a teacher and a friend. For those at the VIP, she was a cautionary bearer of the tale of drunk driving. She was the best wife she could be for her husband. When all was said and done, Joan was happy with the life she was living. She believed she was living her purpose with honor and commitment.

Suddenly, she had to face a new reality, one that included changing all she knew, all she stood for. She had to face that very little that she believed was true, and she had to find a new way to define her mission to change the world. As Joan struggled to make sense of her life, she took a long, hard look at everything she had learned and done since the crash. She thought about everyone she had met, everyone who had come into her life, every accomplishment she had achieved. She thought about how hard Michelle and Teresia had worked with her to help her learn that she had choices about her recovery.

She thought about the work she had done with Marih and Pat to start BIRRDsong, to help those with brain injuries learn that they had a choice about taking back their lives. She thought about the message of the VIP, helping offenders learn they could make a better choice the next time.

Then, suddenly, she saw it. Her life, her reason for being, was about more than a vendetta or finding forgiveness. The common thread of everything she had been through since she came back to life had been about the Power of Choice.

This was Joan's true mission, the purpose and passion she had discovered with Chuck's help in Arizona. She had even told him that in the airport, "My purpose is to make people aware of the gift of choice and that everything they do revolves around choice." But even then she believed her mission revolved around her vendetta against the military. She didn't understand then that there was much, much more to her purpose.

Joan wanted people to know that their choices had results. When the waitress chose to serve the drunken patron just one more beer, her choice mattered. When a customer watched a drunk get into a car and turned the other way, his choice mattered. When the bar owner favored profit over safety, their choice mattered. When a lawmaker voted down a law keeping people safe from drunk drivers, his choice mattered. Joan wanted people to know they had choices and that their choices mattered.

Understanding that her mission revolved around helping people with their choices rather than blaming government agencies made it easier for Joan to move forward with her redefined purpose.

"The target may have been incorrect, but the message was always the same," John says.

"As long as people are aware that this ridiculous nonsense has to stop, and people have to be held accountable I'm happy," Joan says. "Finding out there wasn't an entity to fight, I could be more focused. I didn't have the shadow. I could streamline, do a little bit more, become a little bit more active. I wasn't thinking I had to have the military obsession. My attention went back to the impact panels. When I looked at the audience, I saw people who made a mistake."

Joan was ready to leave her demands for vengeance behind. She wanted to fulfill her purpose, to empower others to make better choices in the first place. Joan finally understood what Susan had been trying to help her see all along. It wasn't about lecturing. It was about finding forgiveness and making a difference.

Now that Joan could see her audience in a different light she, she could also see the man who caused her crash differently. For the first time, she honesty forgave the driver.

"I remember vividly when I couldn't stop crying, because I was thinking, 'It was someone like you who did something like this to someone like me, who did this to my family.' But now I understand. I look at my audience now as people who made a mistake. Some of them are sick, and some of them will re-offend, and I hope nobody gets hurt or loses a life."

Joan called Susan, and they started tweaking Joan's VIP presentations. Elated by Joan's new mindset, Susan eagerly invited her to work on a program specifically designed for teens about the dangers of drunk driving. They both believed that Joan had the street credibility necessary to reach teenagers, who usually blow off advice from adults. With experience as a teenage partier, an adult drunk driver and a victim, Joan was one of the few people who could address it all.

"It was sheer luck I didn't injure or kill someone when I was drinking and driving," she says. "I didn't want anyone to have to go through that."

Susan was happy with Joan's enthusiasm and eagerness to redesign her message, but urged caution. She knew that if not handled carefully, Joan's story could backfire. Instead of a cautionary message, Joan might appear as someone bragging about how she got away with it.

"Everybody says, 'It will never happen to me,'" Susan says. "If presented incorrectly, a message can really mislead teenagers."

"It's about relating," Joan says. "I have to be very, very careful not to give the impression that the bad decisions I made led to this. I'm not a successful drunk driver. I'm successful because I paid a lifelong price, and so did my family. Because of what I did and who I am now, this is what I have, and I have to accept it. What my family had to go through, especially Husband, is bigger than what I'm going through."

Reaching out to educate teenagers on the dangers of drinking and driving was one thing. Telling them personal stories from her past would be another. Susan worried that Joan wasn't ready for how sharing the more embarrassing parts of her life might affect her emotionally. She wanted to make sure that Joan was prepared for how the students would react.

Joan assured her that she was ready because part of the blessing of her new life was her ability to approach her past from a clinical aspect, without being overwhelmed by guilt. This resulted in a matter-of-fact presentation students could hear that came across as fact-based rather than preachy. When it came to her lack of emotions, Joan's brain injury was a gift to her purpose.

"For this change to come about, it had to be so big it almost shut me down. I had to choose this path. I could have just sat in the corner and rocked. I don't know that I could do what I do now if I still had the emotions. I don't know that I would have the mental or emotional or physical strength to go and be effective and try to help people understand that they shouldn't be drinking and driving."

At the same time, Joan is honest about the guilt she carries, even about something that didn't necessarily feel real. "I was able to move on as a speaker without the emotional attachment. Had I had the emotional attachment, that I could have been out there killing people as a drunk driver, I would have never been able to get up there and say, 'Don't do it'," she says.

Standing in front of the teens, Joan showed them they didn't have to be embarrassed by their mistakes. Instead, she used her faded memories to teach how she learned from what she had done. She showed how she could relate to those who had made the same poor choices she once did without drowning in guilt.

"I'm not really even a part of this," she told them. "Often I say, 'Things happen for a reason, and there is a power bigger than all of us. Be willing to know you are not the only speck on the Earth. It's the bigger picture, my family, my friends. Don't do to your family what I could have done to yours.'"

This new approach, about choices, led to immediate success in her ability to reach people everywhere she went. It became common for people to approach her after hearing her speak to thank her for sharing the idea that they had a choice and that they could do better.

"For example, after one panel, a gal who had left the building came back in and hugged me so tight, it was amazing. I'm talking bear hug! She was crying, and I mean REALLY crying, so much so that it was landing on my shoulder. While we were hugging, I gently stroked the back of her head; I asked her if she was OK."

"'No.' She replied"

"'Forgive yourself,'" I told her. "You have to forgive yourself and learn from the experience."

"'I can't,' she said still crying. 'It could have been me that hit you or killed someone else.'"

"'But it wasn't,' I told her. 'And you didn't so you have a second chance, and now it's your choice if you want to learn from the experience and use your second chance to the fullest. Tell your family, your friends; exercise everything you're experiencing right now to save lives. You have that power now.'"

"She finally stopped crying and smiled and said. 'You're amazing, and thank you so much.' I smiled, pointed at her and said. 'You're amazing and now have the power to make change. Go out and do it."

She left with a fist up motion and said, 'I'm doing it, I'm going to do what I can to make sure no one drives after drinking. I'll start being the designated driver."

For Joan, this was what it was all about. These conversations allowed her to leave each presentation knowing she had reached someone, helped them learn they could make better choices. She was finally living her true purpose, and she couldn't have been happier.

"There is a reason I never hurt anyone or myself. I was destined to help more people, and use my stupid stuff that I did as an example, especially with kids. It really is amazing when I think about different things and think, 'Oh my God, this is why!' This is my purpose. I finally realized that I had to make these big mistakes and had to keep going and going because I had a bigger purpose; to save as many lives as possible."

A Question of Time

By 2012, Joan had become a powerful, sought-after speaker. She had a résumé someone without a brain injury would be proud of. She still volunteered at RIO and BIRRDsong, spoke to Dr. Bruce's students and presented on the various Victim Impact Panels with her new message of choice. She spoke to teenagers across Oregon and Southwest Washington and had even been approached by state agencies to speak on the topics of drunk driving and brain injury survival. One of Joan's proudest moments came when Dr. Bruce asked her to speak at the Neuro-Optometric Rehabilitation Association International Conference about how Vision Therapy changed her life.

"That was pretty exciting," she says. "These people were some of Dr. Bruce's mentors. I was speaking to some of the best neuro-optometrists in the world."

In a strange twist of fate, one of the attendees was the neuro-ophthalmologist Joan had seen during her stint at RIO all those years ago. The man who had once told Joan there was no hope for fixing her vision was now watching her speak from the stage about how Dr. Bruce had changed her life with his vision therapy. Joan found it sadly ironic.

Joan wanted to sign up for everything, to accept every engagement, to be at every event. Excited to be out in the world, she said yes to any opportunity that came her way. She thought nothing of scheduling a presentation with Susan in the morning, followed by speaking at a VIP later that night. Then, just as everything was going exactly has she had always hoped, she began to fail.

Joan had once again ignored the physical and mental issues that would take her down if she disregarded them. Only this time, she was letting down people who were counting on her.

Joan just couldn't keep up with the schedule she tried to set for herself. If she spoke on two different panels on Monday, she risked memory lapses on Tuesday. On the days she chose speaking over napping, she would get on stage and not remember what she was there to say. The fatigue would overwhelm her, and her brain would simply shut down. This could lead to a presentation that didn't make any sense.

"It seemed as if I just picked words out of the sky and put them in when I talked," she says. "If I said, 'Because my thought it there,' it would make perfect sense to me at the time. I made up words and used words totally out of context."

Some days she was so tired she couldn't show up at all. This was especially devastating when she had to cancel an engagement with Susan.

"There were a few occasions where she had to cancel doing something at the very last moment, because she couldn't get off the couch," Susan says.

Joan appreciated her understanding, but she knew how hard Susan worked to select people from her volunteer pool to match a scheduled venue. It wasn't easy to replace Joan if she suddenly canceled. Even worse were the times she was so tired that her presentation didn't make any sense, straining the credibility of the organization. Joan knew Susan needed her to be at the top of her game.

Susan never held a cancellation against Joan. She knew it was simply a case of Joan trying to do too much. "I knew when she couldn't do something it wasn't because she had a better offer," Susan says. "It didn't change our friendship whatsoever."

Letting Susan down hurt Joan to the core. Not only had her refusal to take care of herself inconvenienced Susan, she had also missed the opportunity to reach students and help them make better choices. This was her purpose, her passion, her life, and she was blowing it.

Then there was the damage she was doing, once again, to her relationship with her husband. He was the one who lived with the crankiness, the tantrums, the stammering, stuttering and falls that always came with the fatigue. After snapping at him once too often, Joan realized something needed to give.

It all came back to Joan's inability to understand the concept of time. One hour or 12, it was all the same to her. Yesterday, today, tomorrow—for Joan there was no difference. She could easily agree to five two-hour appointments in a row with no concept of the impact it would have.

"You don't translate what two hours is going to do to you," John tried to explain to her repeatedly.

In addition to having guilty feelings over disappointing Susan, Joan also felt guilty about running John hither and yon from one event to another. She rode the LIFT or relied on Susan or

Shawn on a regular basis during the day, but in the evenings, she usually relied on John to get her around town.

"I think about that a lot when I've overbooked and I think to myself, 'Holy Crap, Joan, Husband works nine to 10 hours at a job. You have no right to do this to him. He needs to come home and watch the baseball game.' I try to be conscientious about his time. It's like during baseball season. He loves baseball. He's hooked. So during baseball season, I want him to watch it. If I don't like baseball, I need to shut up and go somewhere else and leave him alone."

John quickly jumps in, denying he felt overworked. "It's not anywhere near that extreme," he says. "Although I agree with you to a point, that's part of the contract of marriage. I get plenty of downtime. It's not a factor."

John may not have felt overwhelmed by the demands of running Joan around, but he did worry about her getting overly tired.

Once again John worked his magic behind the scenes, convincing Joan that she was looking out for him instead of the other way around.

"The way I cope with it is by going through about an hour and half of it and then stopping her and asking her, 'How do you feel? Are you sure you want to do the rest of this stuff? Because I don't.'"

"It's another one of his tricks," Joan says.

Joan knew it was time to go back to the lessons she had learned in the beginning. She needed to stop mentoring everyone else and take some time to mentor herself. She needed to revisit everything

Michelle and Teresia had taught her in RIO and remind herself that although the brain injury was not the driving force in her life, it was a force she couldn't ignore.

She had to remember that respecting the injury was vital to her success. She needed to listen to those around her when they told her she was doing too much and not respond with anger or frustration. Finally, she had to practice what she preached if she wanted to be seen as an example to others.

"When you've spoken both for the Multnomah County Impact Panel and our Impact Panel and then school programs and several things in between, those weeks are more difficult for you than the weeks when you've had your naps and not a 10-hour day." Susan repeatedly explained.

Like a child, Joan had to learn that doing one thing perfectly was better than doing two things halfway. She had to accept, once again, that there were things in her life that would never be right because she had a brain injury. She once again had to acquiesce to John and Shawn's never-ending conspiracies to keep her on track, knowing in her heart they did it out of love. "They are my rudder," Joan says. "Susan is my sail, and Chuck is my boat."

With their guidance, Joan began to monitor her schedule more carefully. She began turning down opportunities regardless of how much she wanted to go play, but she still struggled.

Then came the Mother's Day in 2012 when Joan received invitations to celebrations for both her mom and John's mom. Joan knew she had to make a choice. Which one would she attend? Finally, she turned to John for help.

This simple event set them on a new path of openness and understanding in dealing with how Joan's injury affected their lives. Instead of John manipulating Joan into unconsciously limiting her options, they worked as a couple to find the best solution.

"There are still times I will say, 'I can do it,' and he will shrug and say, 'OK.' Then I will try and fail and have to admit he was right."

"I've finally learned that if I have a speaking engagement during the day not to book stuff that I don't have to. I'll do my best to not even see a doc if I don't have to on those days. With the doctor thing, it's not so much the physical but the mental stress added that has the possibility of interfering with my speaking that evening. The ride on the LIFT can be a long one also, thus adding more fatigue to the day. I want to be on point as much as possible in order to hold my audience in hopes of them learning not to drive impaired."

New Joan

It was 2015 and Joan finally had it all. She had a loving husband and family, reliable friends who cared about her and the knowledge that she was making a difference. The only thing she still really longed for was a sense of normalcy. If only she could, just for a day, be like everyone else. If only she could be Joan first and Joan the survivor second.

One day as Joan and Susan were driving to an event, Susan started laughing at a complaint Joan made about forgetting something. As far as Susan was concerned, Joan was complaining about the kind of memory loss everyone over a certain age grumbles about, not just those with brain injuries. This unexpected response blew Joan away. Accustomed to blaming every bump in the road on her TBI, Joan completely missed that everyone has memory issues once in a while. Susan's random comment offered the idea that Joan might not be that different from everyone else.

As she struggled to work it out, she reviewed what she accepted as true.

Fact: She had a brain injury that required help and guidance with the simplest things.

Fact: She was broken.

New question: What did that mean?

Joan had been a part of the brain injury community for so long that she had lost perspective on the definition of 'normal,' until Susan gave it back to her that day. The more they talked, the more Joan began to see that what she accepted as failings from a TBI were the same age-related challenges everyone has.

"Joan often described things that I related to," Susan says. This was an eye opener for Joan, who for the first time realized that everyone struggles with remembering at some point in their lives. Everyone forgets where they put their keys or the phone number to the pizza place they call five nights a week. It wasn't about having a TBI. It was about forgetting. Just like everyone else did. This strange conversation gave Joan an entirely new view on her life.

Susan's easygoing laugh about memory issues made Joan reevaluate everything she believed about herself. Accepting that forgetting wasn't the end of the world helped reinforce the idea that she could function nearly as well as everyone else. She wasn't necessarily damaged beyond repair. She didn't always have challenges that no one else could relate to. Sometimes, her challenges were just like those of the rest of the world.

"Forgetting my notes for a presentation would usually send me into absolute panic mode, for example. But Susan guided me through the whole thing. She would ask me questions from the audience, and I would start remembering things."

The effect this realization had on Joan was profound. For years, she had defined herself as a survivor of a TBI who was successful but still broken. She couldn't possibly be the same as everyone else. Even her purpose had been based on the concept that her entire life was the result of someone else's choice.

For the first time Joan took a long, hard look at what she had already accomplished. Because of her hard work, many of those with brain injuries realized they had a choice to embrace a *brand new life*. Optometric students had a choice to continue their education and change people's lives through vision therapy. Those who drank had choices not to get in a car. Those who served alcohol had choices not to keep serving. Joan finally began to grasp what others had seen all along. Far from being a damaged woman with a brain injury and loads of guilty history, Joan had become a person who taught about the gift of choices.

With the love of her family and the guidance of such people as Michelle and Teresia, Kathy and Carolyn, Chuck and Susan, Joan had her own choice to make. Would she let her brain injury define her as less than everyone else? Or would she move forward with her purpose and her mission to make the world a better place?

"God said you have to stop existing, and you have to start living. As a result, I am a woman of conviction and someone who has found her purpose," she says. "That purpose is to help other people before they become a victim or cause someone an injury or death from something that is totally preventable. I am a change agent for victims and an acceptance agent for those with brain injuries."

Although the result of the crash was tragic, Shawn believes it served a higher purpose for Joan and those around her. Seeing Joan finally accept all she had accomplished brought Shawn to tears.

"Joan is such a whole person now," Shawn says. "I think we all need some sort of awakening. I think that I'm a better person for having gone through this with Joan and Johnny.

How many times do we get to make a real difference in someone else's life? I feel blessed to have been part of this."

Joan had found the final piece to the puzzle of her life and Providence came running to her once again. "With all the different stupid things I've encountered and done, finally God said, 'OK, now we are done, kick her in the side of the head now, because the story has got to get out, and it has to be big.' With all the serendipitous things that happened, with me being so spiritual, once I found my true path, things began to come my way. Doors are opening that I had no idea existed."

Joan had gone from a woman dying in a hospital bed to a woman who knew who she was and why she was on Earth. She had found her purpose and her passion. She had triumphed over every challenge that had come her way. Her journey and her life would never be easy, but she was a whole functioning human being who was ready to walk through any door yelling at the top of her lungs, "I can make better choices and so can you!" She was finally whole and she knew exactly who to thank.

The Marriage of a Lifetime

Joan knows, and tells anyone who will listen, that she wouldn't be the success she is without the help of her husband, John. Although on the surface, it was all about her journey, her recovery and her purpose, she knows that without him, she would never have gotten here. She might be the one making a difference in public, but he made it possible. As Joan's popularity has grown, a surprised John has found himself in the limelight right along with her.

Pleased as he is by Joan's success, John is still uncomfortable at the attention. He doesn't understand it. Why are people looking at him? Why is he such an important part of her story? Why do people come up to him after the VIP panels and compliment him for his role as a husband? Why are people so surprised by his dedication to his wife?

"I guess it seems kind of weird to me, too, because that's not what I grew up with," he says. John's biological father was often absent, and even when he was home, he was alternately distant and verbally abusive to the entire family.

"He was in the Army when my parents got married, and when I was 3 or 4, we moved to Seattle without him. The idea of loyalty was not something I grew up with, so maybe my loyalty to Joan is just the boomerang effect my childhood had on me."

So how does he answer those who asked him why he stayed?

"I don't understand the question," a bewildered John replies. "I truly don't understand. People have told me that relationships break up, marriages break up, because of things like this. But no, it never occurred to me that leaving was an option. It never occurred to me not to stick around. That just wasn't an option that ever entered my head. You don't just walk out. You don't just walk away."

John never felt the need to leave because when he looks at Joan he still sees the woman he fell in love with. Even with all the physical and mental challenges after the crash, the Joan he knew was still there, deep inside. She was the same person Kathy knew back in high school, the one who tried to hide from the world behind an alcoholic facade. Joan didn't fool him then and she doesn't fool him now.

"I think the brain injury sort of scraped away a lot of the nonsense, and she could go back to the basic Joan. I saw the humor and the compassion for other people that had been obvious to me from when I first met her. The TBI allowed her to become the person she wanted to be, the person everyone else knew was there."

Joan says, "I had never thought about it that way, but it's so true. I didn't have to put on a falseness. I was just a bare core, learning how to do everything again, so it was like, 'We are going to start from scratch.' It allowed me to really see, to give a whole different value to life in general. It gave me a whole different approach. It made me much less self-destructive. I was going through life just existing. Then God kicked me in the side of the head and said, 'Start living!'"

Many of those around Joan believe the crash was a necessary event. Without it, she would never have become the person she was meant to be. Even Joan believes this is a second chance to do it right, regardless of the cost. But what about John? Was it worth it to him? Was this new life a better life? Was the crash necessary?

"That's an unfair question," he says. "I don't think this was necessary, no. I think we both would have turned it around without the crash. I don't think we *needed* this, no. Because both of us were on a path that was not sustainable, we would have gotten there on our own."

He does admit that the crash stopped him in his tracks, causing him to reevaluate his life. "It sort of forced me to hold a mirror up to myself and ask myself some questions about where I was going as opposed to where I wanted to go."

Where he wanted to go was forward with Joan, regardless of their challenges. As far as he was concerned, problems were inevitable in any marriage. It's how husbands and wives work through those problems that count. John believes that although the brain injury brought a new layer of issues, they weren't insurmountable ones.

"Maybe some of the normal problems people have in their marriages are magnified by the injury. At the same time, many of the problems couples face in a normal marriage are less important, because we have perspective."

Seeing Joan in that hospital bed and then watching her fight her way back gave John all the patience he would ever need to keep things in perspective for living with Joan and her brain injury. At the same time, he is quick to point out that wasn't the only reason they were successful in keeping their marriage together. He believes much of their success came from the life experience they had each gained from their checkered pasts. Joan might have had the more dramatic history, but John is the first to admit that she wasn't the only one with growing pains. He had his own issues in his younger days, living a life that was almost as colorful as Joan's.

"I had issues with anger and alcohol in my 20s, but then I grew up. We both got lucky," John says. "If we had met in our mid to late 20s, this relationship wouldn't have worked."

He believes the chance to experience all the ups and downs life could offer may have made them uniquely qualified to weather the storm of a brain injury and still hold their marriage together.

"I think it's a maturity issue. It took us a long time to find each other. I was 43 when we got married, and Joan was 35. We had been friends for years and had been married for seven years when all this took place. When it comes to a marriage surviving, you have to ask yourself: How mature was the relationship? How mature were the people in the relationship? How healthy was the relationship before the incident?" John says.

Some differences have always existed in their basic personalities. John has always been the calm, controlled, reserved bulldog to Joan's exuberant hummingbird. He was initially drawn to Joan's excitable and rather frantic nature, just as she was drawn to his stability and quietness. This opposites-attract relationship left John uniquely prepared to deal with the wild mood swings that can come with a brain injury, because he had been dealing with them all along. Unlike many couples who might find themselves in the same situation, John didn't have to fundamentally change who he was to cope with the changes in his wife.

"I've always been pretty much who I am now," he says. "Even today, she will react to something, and I'll make one comment and wait for her to calm down and come back to the middle. And she eventually does."

"Like, what do you mean?" Joan interrupts.

John reminds Joan about her most recent reaction to an unpleasant event. He had hired a tree trimmer who cut a tree much shorter than Joan was expecting, and she was unhappy with the results.

"She was just pissed!" John says. "It took Joan 45 minutes to an hour to come back and see that it was reasonable. But I'm used to it. It made me crazy in the first few years, but now I'm used to it."

As Joan listened to John describe her response, she was amazed. She hadn't realized that even 12 years later she still had such obvious and lengthy tantrums.

"Don't worry," he reassured her with a smile. "You always come back. I don't try to reason with you. I just wait."

"Really? I always come back? Wow."

"Joan has no concept that she is temperamental," he says.

"What does that word mean?" she challenges.

"It means your emotions are extreme."

Listening to John discuss her behavior upset Joan, who had assumed she had finally gained the upper hand on her emotions. She doesn't quite understand that although she has improved tremendously from her days in RIO her outbursts are still fairly common. Most of the people around her are so used to them that they ignore them. It's just Joan being Joan.

"It may have been aggravated by the brain injury, but it's always been part of who she is," John says. "She's emotional and excitable, and there are plusses and minuses there. When she gets happy, she's *really* happy. When she's sad, she's *really* sad. When she's mad, she's *really* mad. Joan still has little in the way of a filter for her emotions."

"I do know at times I react so quickly that I don't give a shit. This is how I feel!" Joan quickly says, proving John's point.

"You can be intimidating," he tells her.

"Oh really?" she answers, surprised. "I had no idea!"

Joan still struggles to contain her emotions, but the days of screaming for attention are long gone. Now she can identify the consequences of her feelings and actions and respond accordingly. Given enough time, that is.

"With the tree thing, John came in and said, 'Don't get mad at Ray for cutting the tree, get mad at me.' Then I had to realize that the consequence was I was going to hurt my husband's feelings if I didn't get my temper tantrum under control. I'm trying to become a little more self-aware. Why am I doing what I'm doing? But in that process it's after the fact, so then I have to use it as a lesson. A lot of times I don't see it ahead of time."

John loves that Joan is still learning and accomplishing goals, no matter how long it takes. He estimates that Joan is about 60% aware that she has a brain injury, and he is grateful for that. He would gladly take a moody and temperamental Joan at 60% any day over the no-hope Joan back in the intensive care in Utah. He has his wife back and is proud of her accomplishments.

John reluctantly admitted it was tiring to always keep his guard up in the early years, and he is happy to have a Joan who is a bit more self-sufficient. "I still do it, but I'm not completely paranoid all the time," he says.

Over time, he has even become more comfortable with Joan's tendency to wander. "If you get confused and don't know where you are or where to go, there are always lots of people to ask," he reminds her regularly.

"But here is the difference between now and 10 years ago," John says: "Now, I know she isn't going to get hurt. She's going to stop and go, 'Oh, wait a minute, what am I doing?' and wait for us to find each other. Before that wasn't the case."

At the same time, it is hard for John to take any credit for Joan's growth. "To say that I got her to that point is to imply she didn't do anything by herself," John says.

Joan says, "My brain injury forced him, and allowed him, to see what he was completely capable of doing for someone else, for someone he loves. He had to not be the quiet guy in the corner so much. John was always quiet and reserved, but now he had to be vocal. He had to get out there and be present. He had to be forthright."

"That's what the crash did for John. Before, if someone was running toward me, John would pull me behind him. Now, he steps in front of me with his hand up and says, 'STOP!'"

"I disagree," John says. "It goes back to what we were talking about originally. As far as I'm concerned, I haven't done anything different. I'm not saying I'm the same person, but I don't feel like I've done anything significantly different."

One thing John will accept is the knowledge that Joan benefits when she brags about him. Even when it brings him into the unwanted glare of the spotlight, it's worth it if it helps her.

"It's something she needs to do. Whatever discomfort there is for me is small and temporary. If that's what she needs me to do that's fine. I have no problem with it. If it came to be that *Ellen* or *The Today Show* called and wanted us to come on, I would deal with it. My preference would be to not be on camera, but if I saw that it was necessary for Joan, I would do it."

After all this time, John still finds himself in the position of defending his motives and morals. Some of those who can't understand the depth of his love and dedication find it inconceivable. They accuse him of staying in the marriage out of a sense of duty, guilt or depression—charges he vehemently denies.

"No, it's just that's what you do in a relationship. At least, that's the way it seems to me. I'm human, and you can't avoid bitterness from time to time, but overall no, I'm not guilty or depressed. It's a waste of time. The evidence that I am not would be how I handled my drinking behavior. I went this way and not the other way. If I was wallowing in guilt, I would have gone the other way. You do what you have to do. People will read into it what they want to read into it."

"I will admit that there are times when I think about how our lives would be different if this had never had happened. I think about how different things would be if we had been compensated. But I'm not going to dwell on it. You have to deal with things as they are."

"I never said I was OK with the crash. But I'm happy with my life. I hope that makes sense to people, but I don't really care if it does," he says. "We all have our *normal*. For me, this is normal. It's been an interesting journey. It's never boring. Even with everything, it's still fun. Joan's personality is to have fun, and I can't help but have fun because I'm there with her."

Normal, interesting, never boring and still fun—it's the words they use to describe the marriage of two lifetimes. The second chance they were given may not have been the one they would have chosen, but the life they now have, injury and all, is one they would never give up.

Joan's New Life

"What do I want the reader to take away on Joan?" she asks. "Perseverance is an absolute must in anything. Be true to yourself. Do not listen to naysayers. You have to be true to yourself. Find support. Associate with people who encourage you and don't discourage you. Have faith. Never give up. Never give up."

Joan understands not everyone with a TBI will have a recovery like hers, but she believes her survival is directly related to her mission to help others however she can.

"In 2012, BIRRDsong became what I envisioned so many years ago. It had an executive board dedicated to taking it to the national level, was connecting people with TBIs all around the area and has now become part of the larger Brain Injury Connections NW."

Joan still speaks for the VIP panels for Oregon Impact and Trauma Nurses Talk Tough. She can be seen all over Oregon and Washington sharing her message of making a better choice.

Grateful to the therapists she once despised at RIO, today, Joan is an active participant in their marketing campaigns. Her smiling face is found on brochures, DVDs, websites, anything they can use. Visitors to RIO can even find a huge photo of her hanging at the entrance as an example of one of their many success stories.

Joan works with graduate students throughout the metro area, in fields ranging from optometry to speech therapy, helping them understand the world from the view of someone with a brain injury. Her blog (www.Joanwins.com) is filled with letters from students thanking her for showing them life outside the textbook.

Joan continues to speak to students at middle and high schools throughout Oregon and Southwest Washington, offering her message of better choices for a better life.

In February 2014, Joan received The Saint Mary's Academy award in the category of Overcoming Adversity. She was nominated by alumni and family, who suggested Joan as a recipient based on her remarkable achievements. Past winners of the St. Mary's Academy Award include Patricia Haslach, U.S. ambassador to Ethiopia, and Assistant U.S. Attorney for the District of Oregon Leah Bolstad.

Joan's latest adventure, with the help of Chuck Goetschel and Toastmasters, is taking her message of choice to entirely new audiences through motivational speaking.

It wasn't until Joan read her story for the first time that she grasped the idea that she is a living miracle, and saw how the path she has chosen led to her accomplishments. When Dr. Welling, the neurosurgeon who initially saw her in Utah, was asked how he thought she survived and recovered his answer was simple. "There is no explanation for Joan," he said.

Happy with the life she is living, she no longer needs an explanation. She's too busy teaching others how to make toast.

Joan's Words of Wisdom

- *Toothpaste does NOT make a good exfoliating cream.*
- *If you want to safely exit a bathroom, open the door before you walk through the doorway!*
- *Before toasting an English muffin, check that you have removed the toast from the day before.*
- *When making egg salad for sandwiches, it works best to peel the eggs.*
- *When picking up the necklace I dropped today, I found the towel I lost days ago!*
- *The paper that's put between sliced cheese has a potential for adding confusion to the biting process.*
- *You know it's time for a nap when the buzzer for the dryer goes off and you open your oven.*

My Journey: A Thank You to All from Joan

They say it takes a village. I say "Sometimes, it takes an entire country." The journey I've been on since June 12, 1999, has taken many turns, dips and some paths that were somewhat easy to follow. I never would have been able to accomplish any of this without the love and support of so many.

Of all these people, there is one person who I could not have made this journey without. That's my husband John, who I lovingly call, "Husband." His strength, patience and unconditional love took me out of some scary and dark times, allowing God's brilliant light and love to shine on my face and carry me through. He always held my head upward even when I felt too weak to do so. He was, is and always will be My Rock! How he can take the most complex things and make them easy for me to understand is a simple way to explain how he helped the woman he fell in love with, find the woman I am now and rejoice in every achievement along the way. Even when it's complex as learning to make toast. Husband, I couldn't love you more. You ARE my life.

My parents and sisters have been relentless in allowing me to trip, stumble, fall and even laugh with me when I was laughing at myself. They were teaching me to just keep on keepin' on—all while setting up an invisible force field with their love and caring, making sure someone always had an eye on me (I tend to just kinda "do" things) and that I was safe. Thank you, Mama, Daddy, Tina, Rita, Ann, Linda, Lisa, Patty,

Shawn and Kim. I love you with everything I'm made of, most of which is pasta!

Among the most gifted and dedicated professionals in this world, I've been blessed with the best. They not only healed my broken body, they touched my heart, leaving their spirit of compassion and healing my broken spirit. They all were instrumental in guiding me down a path, that was far from the yellow brick road, but my own road and turning my misery into a ministry.

To Dr. Blake Welling, the gifted neurosurgeon who saved my life in the wee hours of June 12, 1999, I could never thank you enough. You gave new meaning to "birthday" when I turned 42 lying in a coma on my June 13, birthday. It was surely God working through your fine hands, brilliant mind and brain that allowed that to happen. My wings didn't fit, and you made it possible I keep shopping for a new pair. I look forward to calling you every year on my birthday, as I have done for years now, just to say "thank you for giving me another one." Celebrate birthdays my friends. God gave them to us for a reason!

There aren't enough words in the human language to describe Dr. Bruce who I love like the brother. His God-given gift allowed him to give me back my world. Because of the damage to my brain, everything I once knew had literally fallen apart or I saw so many of them I could make no sense of it. He was able to take my visual world that had just been rocked to its core and give me back my sense of normalcy.

This is his purpose that he pursues with intense passion. Patients who have Dr. Bruce of NW EyeCare

Professionals as their Behavioral Optometrist are blessed to say the least. Once Dr. Bruce touches your head, heart and soul, he doesn't let go. He has changed my life forever, and for the better as I go out in the world and try to emulate him. He is not only my hero; he is a source of my strength. His wife, Nancy, is also a true inspiration to me. Without her even knowing so, she has taught me how love and respect myself with everything I do. Your beautiful children are a reflection of your love, and I cherish that you've brought them into my life. Thank you, Dr. Bruce, Nancy, Justin and Ally. As my journey continues, I will strive to touch lives as you all do on a daily basis!

Everyone needs a good cuckoo doctor at one time or another. I'll need Dr. Cole for the rest of my life, and I'm grateful that he's here for me. I would never have understood the magnitude or scope of my injury if it hadn't been for him explaining it to me in a language I could understand. Simple is always better, especially in the brain-injured world. Thank you, Dr. Cole. You've made my life easier for me to enjoy while giving respect to the injury that reinvented Joan.

My speaking journey would have never taken the wonderful turns it has had it not been for Chuck Goetschel. Chuck was the influence allowing me to see my purpose. Medically, my return from near death is not the norm. I was put here on earth to make a difference, not to exist, but to live and touch lives in the process.

My thanks, love and tons of hugs go out to Carolyn Martin and Kathy Richard. My words would have never seen their way to paper, much less an audience if not for these two wonderful women; women who I have the delight and honor to call friends. They took the time from their busy schedules to mentor and give me the extra push onto a stage, reminding me to speak from my heart and not my head.

There is so much I can say about my best friend, Susan Lehr, and not enough paper. Susan was my first friend after the crash; she got the unabridged edition of Joan. In other words, she got me raw and, at times, unedited. I thank God daily for her patience, perseverance and continued love. She met the "Joan" I was still trying to get to know and has never wavered in her loyalty and friendship. Words could never tell you, Susan, just how much I love you and what an impact you made in my heart and soul. I continue to strive to keep making you proud of me.

There was a time when Oregon Impact needed new leadership and in stepped Janelle Lawrence to take on the challenge. Janelle not only took on the role as Oregon Impact's leader, she stepped into my heart as well. She's there for me day or night, just a phone call away if I need anything or simply want to talk. She bends over backward to make sure I'm present at as many events as possible, making sure I have the opportunity to impact and influence people into making better choices.

When you need the best and most dedicated moderator of the Victim Impact Panels—a man I've had the pleasure of calling friend—to explain why impaired driving is not only against the law, but changes lives forever, Judge Gregory Silver is the man for the job. With a never-ending respect for others and a deep caring to make a change in people's perception of bad choices, Judge Silver steps up to the plate and always hits a home run. He has made me a better speaker by being more conscious of people and the fact most people simply made a mistake with their bad choice. Thank you Greg, you are a blessing in my life and the lives of others.

It would be best to thank the author of my biography, Kelly Sharp. I met Kelly years ago when I was still wearing a helmet, sporting a walker, and sounded and looked drunk when I talked or walked. She didn't stare at me like I was a freak show or could be the *star* of a book someday. She'll tell you she watched me navigate a world where she, thank God, didn't have a map. Stunned and somewhat in awe at times, Kelly saw someone who recovered from a horrific crash only to call this "new normal" my world. She saw a spirit that she was inspired to tell the world about.

I am grateful to everyone who was in my life or has come into my life once again. Every one of you has left a permanent mark on my soul and written your names on my heart. I take those marks with me, cherish and hold them tightly. At times, I need to pull them out in order to put one foot in front of the other. I may never run again; however, with my head held high and my arms outstretched, I will continue to live a purpose-filled life and make a difference in this world, one small step at a time.

500 Words and a Kickstarter campaign

It was supposed to be a 500-word essay for a contest I wanted to enter on medical miracles. But the more Joan and I talked, the more I realized this story went far beyond a car crash. At its heart it was a love story about a woman who survived the impossible and the man who stood by her side. It wanted to be told, and it chose me to it write it. And I did - with the help of friends and family and the kindness of strangers:

- My husband, Ward Muehlberg, who encouraged and believed in me every step of the way.
- John and Joan, who trusted me to write their story and who changed my life for the better.
- Jo Arrowsmith, Carrie Kwiatkowski, Ildi Lane, Sara Mottau, Roberta Muehlberg, Karen Murphy, Diana Phillips and Shawn VanDoren who read draft after draft and never failed to find something I could use to make the story better.
- Keri Losavio, editor extraordinaire, for all of the suggestions and blue ink (thank you for not using red!)
- All the people in Joan's life who shared their stories of her incredible life.

And, of course, my Kickstarter backers who helped bring this story from a dream to a reality. Without them it may have languished forever in the back of a drawer.

- Cynthia Thurber; John Miller; Oregon Impact
- Janelle Lawrence; Donna Morrison; Shawn "Nadine" VanDoren
- Noe Betancourt; Paul Gallaugher; Chuck Goetschel; Heidi A Kleist; Kathy and George Kuiawa; Carrie Kwiatkowski; Sue Larson; Dr. Rik Lemoncello; Lorraine Linder-Skach; Carolyn Martin; Kim Miller Yamashita; Catherine Mindolovich; Kathy Richard; Felipe Santiago Soriano; Ernie and Jody Santos; Ronald D. Scott; Connie Shipley; Greg and Dale Silver; Will Toogood; Mary Weiler; Katie Yates; Adam.
- Chip Allen; C Bullock; Debbie Domby-Hood; Jeff Hartson; Sarah Jurhs; Joshua, Kelsey & Adriana McDougall; Jan and Rick Roise; Jane Ulvan; Paula Westhusing

Thank you all,

Kelly

A Few of Joan's Favorite Websites

Joan Miller
www.joanwins.com

Kelly Sharp
www.kellymsharp.com

BEST – Brain Energy Support Team
www.brainenergysupportteam.org

BIC-NW – Brain Injury Connections NW
www.bicnw.org

CBIRT- Center on Brain Injury Research & Training
www.cbirt.org

Chuck Goetschel
www.chuckgoetschel.com/

Dr. Bruce Wojciechowski, NW EyeCare Professionals
www.doctorbruce.net

Legacy Health
Healing Gardens Horticultural Therapy

Mothers Against Drunk Driving
www.maad.org

National Brain Injury Association of America
www.biausa.org

Oregon Impact
www.oregonimpact.org

Legacy Good Samaritan Hospital
<u>Rehabilitation Institute of Oregon (RIO)</u>

Who Am I to Stop It?
<u>www.whoamitostopit.com</u>

*A documentary film of how art brings brain injury survivors
out of isolation bringing to light the power of one's own gifts
helping to adapt to living with a brain injury*